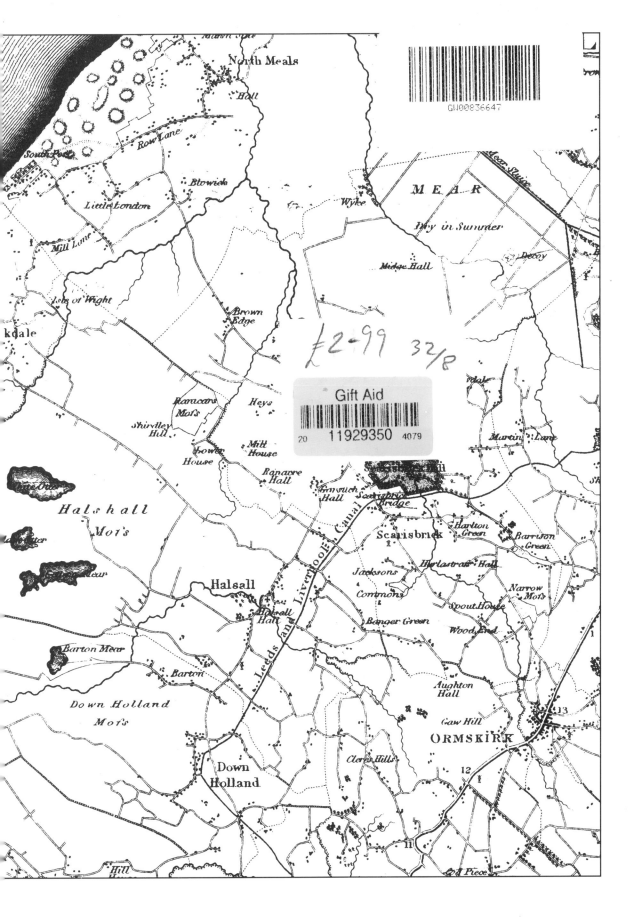

North Meals

Hall

Row Lane

South Port

Blowick

Little London

Mill Lane

Isle of Wight

kdale

Brown Edge

M E A R

Dry in Summer

Wyke

Midge Hall

Decoy

£2·99   32/8

Heys

Raracans Mof's

Shirdley Hill

Lower House

Mill House

Ranavre Hall

Little Don

Halshall

Mof's

eter

Mear

Halsall

Halsall Hall

Barton Mear

Barton

Down Holland

Mof's

Leeds and Liverpool Canal

Ormsuch Hall

Scarisbrick Bridge

Scarisbrick

Harlton Green

Barrison Green

Harlastrat Hall

Martin Lane

dale

Sh

Jacksons

Commons

Narrow Mof's

Spout House

Banger Green

Wood End

Aughton Hall

Gaw Hill

ORMSKIRK

13

Cleves Hills

12

Down Holland

11

Hill H

God Piece

SOUTHPORT
A Pictorial History

Cambridge Hall, engraving, 1872.

SOUTHPORT
A Pictorial History

Harry Foster

Phillimore

1995

Published by
PHILLIMORE & CO. LTD.,
Shopwyke Manor Barn, Chichester, West Sussex

ISBN 0 85033 966 9

Printed and bound in Great Britain by
BIDDLES LTD.
Guildford, Surrey

List of Illustrations

Frontispiece: Cambridge Hall, engraving, 1872

Acknowledgements

In preparing this book I am grateful to have had the opportunity to work within the fellowship of the Birkdale and Ainsdale Historical Research Society. Led by Sylvia Harrop, the members are Reg Baxter, Terence Burgess, Audrey Coney, Joan Diggle, Rene Merritt, Peggy Ormrod, Pat Perrins and Bill Pick. Although the book owes much to their collaboration and support, the interpretations are my own, and I must be held responsible.

For the provision of illustrations, I should like to thank: the Royal Commission on Historical Monuments in England; Mr. Tony Wray, Keeper of Art Galleries and Museums, who is responsible for the collection at Sefton's Botanic Gardens' Museum; Mr. Philip King, Sefton's Chief Tourism and Attractions Officer; Mr. K. Hall, formerly Lancashire County Archivist; Miss Janet Smith formerly Liverpool City Archivist; Miss Margaret Proctor of the Merseyside Record Office; Edge Hill College Geography Department; Miss Chris Ainsbury; Mrs. Carole Bamber; Mr. Alan Bond; Mrs. Ann Coates; Messrs. Mark Chatterton, Martin Connard, Adrian Fletcher, Peter Gibb, Bill Marsden, Alan Marshall, John Masters, Arthur Pedlar, Chris Perrins, John Robinson; Mrs. Jean Rivett, Messrs. Ian Simpson, Tim Timmerman; and Mrs. Hannah Wignall.

Finally, thanks are due to: Sylvia Harrop, the Society's Publication Editor; Pat Perrins, the Society Secretary; Neil McDowall, John Robinson, and especially Alan R. Whittaker, for the photographic work; Chris Driver, for computer assistance; and my wife Thelma, for help in so many ways.

HARRY FOSTER
FEBRUARY 1995

Introduction

In 1992, Southport, a seaside residential town and resort with some 85,000 inhabitants, celebrated its bi-centenary. Like Blackpool, St Annes and Morecambe, Southport is a comparatively new name that is not to be found on early maps. It had its beginnings as the favoured location for late 18th-century bathers who, following the contemporary fashion for sea-bathing, were visiting the village of Church Town in the parish of North Meols. By the late 19th century, Southport had emerged as the 'Queen of Lancashire resorts', but its destiny was to become a socially advantaged residential town, a garden city. It was aptly described as a monument representing the energy and industry of Lancashire people.[1]

The first chapter gives a largely sequential account of the opportunist, even haphazard, beginnings of the town, a theme well rehearsed in a line of local histories, although the emphasis given here to cause and effect may have some freshness.[2]

Chapter Two is concerned with the rapid growth, after 1842, of Southport as a seaside resort and then as a residential town. The respective rôles of the landowners, the local authorities, entrepreneurs, institutions and philanthropists are examined, and the changing nature of the emerging town analysed. The tensions and contests between different interests which shaped the town during this period are less well known.

The final chapter deals with Southport following the amalgamation with its suburb Birkdale and its designation as a County Borough. The increased functions and responsibilities being given to local government during this period are shown to change the balance of power in the town. There is also a new balance to be struck between Southport the resort, Southport the commuter base, and Southport a place of residence and employment.

The illustrations are grouped to reflect the chapters and the captions are intended to supplement the text.

Notes

1. *Bootle Times*, 13 March 1888.
2. E. Bland, *Annals of Southport and District* (1903), W.T. Bulpit, *Notes on Southport and District* (1908), F.A. Bailey, *A History of Southport* (1955). Much of the data for this, the most detailed and measured history of the town, was collected by F.H. Cheetham. P. Aughton, *North Meols and Southport* (1988). This account includes an emphasis on significant individuals and family reconstruction.

Chapter One
The Beginnings: 1792-1842

The parish of North Meols was situated on the Lancashire coast between the Mersey and Ribble estuaries. Prior to the 19th century, this corner of south-west Lancashire was comparatively isolated from the remainder of the county. Immediately to the north stretched the wide expanse of marsh and mud of the Ribble estuary. The landward approach was constrained by mosses and meres, and confined to tracks on the higher ground. To the south a belt of sandhills formed 'a barrier to ordinary communication'.[1]

Time had passed the area by. Using Bishop Gastrell's survey of 1720, it has been estimated that the parish of North Meols, consisting of the Townships of North Meols and Birkdale, had a population of under one thousand two hundred.[2] The natives, living in thatched low-slung cottages of clamstaff and daub, depended for their meagre livelihood on farming, fishing, and hand-loom weaving, many practising a combination of the three. Church Town (later Churchtown) was the principal village of North Meols, the site of the ancient parish church of St Cuthbert's, the manorial hall, and a mill. Outlying hamlets of the parish are shown on Yates' map of 1786. To the north stood Crossens, on an 'island' of high ground, 'untouched by floods' or tides.[3] Marshside was to the seaward of Church Town village, on land progressively reclaimed from the sea. Blowick lay astride the main track to the interior, on low-lying peaty soil, about a mile to the south of Church Town. Row Lane led from Church Town to the scattered cottages of the sandhill region, marked 'Horse Houses'. Despite the inhospitable appearance of this area, parish registers reveal that Horse Houses (or South Hawes) was surprisingly well populated. Further south lay the scattered farms and cottages of Birkdale.[4] Although Church Town contained the seats of the two Lords of the Manor—the Heskeths and the Bolds—at the end of the 18th century neither family lived in the neglected halls in this unproductive portion of their estates. Roger Hesketh had married into the Fleetwood family of Rossall Hall in 1733, thereby acquiring extensive estates in the Fylde and also the status of leading gentry. The family became resident at Rossall Hall. The Bolds, who had been leading gentry for many years, had their family seat at Bold Hall, near to Warrington. The rector was also an absentee, living in the inland market town of Ormskirk. The church and school were in a relatively dilapidated condition and the upper and middle classes were not represented in the resident population.[5]

Sea-bathing appears to have been a feature of local festivals in North Meols. On Big and Little Bathing Sundays local residents and farm labourers from inland villages took advantage of the broad beach for sea-bathing. During the 18th century, sea-bathing and sea-air gained acceptance by many doctors as being therapeutic. These views and the curtailment of continental travel by the French war, contributed to seaside holidays in England becoming fashionable. Visitors seeking sea-bathing at North Meols initially came to stay in the two old inns—*The Black Bull* (later the *Hesketh Arms*) and the *Griffin* (later the *Bold Arms*)—at Church Town. With silt from the Ribble Estuary marring the nearest beach to Church Town, much better bathing conditions were available some two miles to the south, in front of the sandy wastes of South Hawes. It seems that William Sutton, nicknamed 'The Duke', who was an enterprising landlord of the *The Black Bull*, transported visitors from Church Town to this superior beach. In 1792, he built a temporary bathing house for the convenience of his visitors. This roughly constructed shelter was at the southern end of a long marshy hollow between the sand hills, that is now Lord Street. The venture was so successful that six years later Sutton obtained a lease for six acres from the landowner, Miss Bold, and moved with his family to a permanent hotel, *South-Port Hotel*, which he built alongside the bathing shelter.

Sutton has been widely fêted as the founder of Southport, but the founding of a town is a difficult concept. It seems likely that the cottagers of South Hawes received visitors in their tiny homes, prior to the building of *Sutton's Hotel*. New residents were also attracted to the area. The first new house was built by Mrs. Sarah Walmesley, a widow from Wigan, in 1797, the year before Sutton moved into residence. Mrs. Walmesley's Belle Vue cottage, in which she received paying guests, was situated immediately to the south of Sutton's bathing house, on land leased from Mr. Hesketh. When Sutton built his shelter in 1792, he certainly made a significant contribution to the development of Southport and it is this date which his fellow townspeople later chose to celebrate as the founding of the town. Even less clear than the question of foundation is that of how Southport (initially South Port) gained its name. The most popular explanation is that it was so christened, during a 'convivial' evening following the opening of *Sutton's Hotel*, by Dr. Barton, an Ormskirk enthusiast for sea-bathing, who was one of the new hamlet's earliest inhabitants, erecting Nile Cottage between Belle Vue and the sea.

Further new dwellings followed to cater for the increasing number of visitors and as early as 1809 a diarist, Ellen Weeton, the governess to an Upholland family, recorded: 'Many people of some consequence and fashion ... have resorted there during the last two years. It is becoming a fashionable watering place'.[6] Indeed, the neglected Bold House (in Manor Road, Churchtown) had been rebuilt in 1802 so that the Bold family could take advantage of the bathing. It was the Bolds who helped popularise Southport with neighbouring gentry and establish it as a locally fashionable resort.

The opening of the Leeds and Liverpool canal in 1774 conferred an early advantage on Southport over its potential rivals as a Lancashire coast watering place. From Liverpool, the canal made its way north following the contours. Thus it ran behind Southport, with the Red Lion Bridge at Scarisbrick being only some five miles inland from the town. Visitors were brought by packet boat to Scarisbrick and thence to North Meols by carriage or cart. They came from inland Lancashire rather than from Liverpool, which had its own bathing beaches.

Despite deferential claims to the contrary, the part played by the landowners in the beginnings of Southport appears to have been slight. When the demand arose for leases for building at South Hawes, the two landowners, linked by marriage, agreed to divide this previously ignored wasteland between them. The new settlers paid very modest rentals for the plots on which they built their marine villas in the position they chose, with little interference from the landowners. It was largely nature, in the shape of aspect, brooks, marsh and sandhills, which dictated where the buildings might be erected.

Initially dubbed a 'folly', the Duke's *South-Port Hotel* was the focus of continuing development. A cluster of marine villas—Willow Cottage, West Hill, Belmont Cottage, South Hill, Nile Villa, and Beach Cottage—soon filled the gap between *Sutton's Hotel* and the Birkdale boundary, where development came to an abrupt stop. The Township of Birkdale was the property of a third family—the Blundells of Ince—who, at this time, had no interest in the urban development of this part of their estate. Thus, as the hamlet could not follow a conventional pattern and expand to the south and west, developers looked north to the broad marshy valley down which the donkey carts had brought the original visitors from Church Town.

A second hotel, *The Union*, was built in 1805, whilst Wellington Terrace, built by a consortium of Wigan businessmen and still present on the inland side of Lord Street, marks the beginning of ribbon development back along Lord Street (originally in the plural, Lords Street, in recognition of the two Lords of the Manor). By 1820 cottages lined both sides of Lord Street's south end. The 88-yard gap between the building lines has been cited as the product of thoughtful planning.[7] It appears that it was more probably a result of an anxiety to avoid the frequently waterlogged marshy ground along the centre of the valley,[8] and also, perhaps, an attempt 'to accommodate the higgledy-piggledy buildings erected by the original squatter-leaseholders'.[9] The frequently repeated assertion from *The Victoria County History*, that Lord Street was created by an Act of Parliament of 1825 is a result of confusion with Lord Street in Liverpool.[10] After early haphazard development, a series of cross-roads and roads parallel to Lord Street gave depth and definition to the hamlet. The regular layout again suggests careful planning; this appears, however, to be a by-product of the two landowners having partitioned the 'waste' ground into rectangular plots, which they divided between them.

A list of occupations given by Glazebrook, whose guide books provide an important source for the early history of Southport, demonstrates the dependence of the new hamlet on sea-bathing. In the 1826 edition, in addition to the inns, 59 of the 107 householders are recorded as receiving visitors.[11] Amenities for visitors and residents were quick to follow. Robert Hesketh gave the site for Christ Church, Southport's first church, built at the northern extremity of the hamlet in 1821, whilst both landowners contributed to its construction. Two years later an Independent Chapel was built in Eastbank Lane, on a plot also given by Robert Hesketh, at the corner of what was to become Chapel Street.[12] Other modest amenities shown on an 1824 map included: baths, a makeshift theatre, a billiard room, a post office, wine vaults and a repository. The 1820s saw a rapid increase in the number of houses built in Southport. Entrepreneurs were encouraged to invest in developing the resort. Progressively the cottages on the seaward side of Lord Street were converted into shops, leaving domestic dwellings on the 'garden side' of the road. A third inn, the *Hesketh Arms* (later the *Scarisbrick Arms*), was built in 1821. An Assembly and News Room, vital for a fashionable resort, was built in 1829, at the corner of Lord Street and London Street. Linear development continued northwards along Lord Street, to where the old carriage track turned inland down Manchester Road. In confirmation of Southport's emerging status, the *Bold Arms*, a superior class of hotel, was opened at this north end of Lord Street in 1832.

The success of the infant town was sufficient to encourage people to invest in even more ambitious schemes. One of the first ventures was the making of a sea-wall and Promenade. This project, started in 1835, was designed to serve the dual function of offering protection to the outer sandhills from the spring tides, thus allowing property to be built, and to provide the watering place with a Promenade overlooking the beach. It is significant that the landowner, Peter Hesketh Fleetwood, 'encouraged' the venture, without investing in it. As will be seen, this was in marked contrast to the active rôle he played in building sea defences at Fleetwood. A second company, Southport New Baths Company, was formed to build baths and to extend the Promenade northwards from Nevill Street, on land leased from Sir Henry Bold Hoghton. The Royal Victoria Baths were opened in 1839. Two years later *Claremont House* was opened as a high-class hotel and quickly attracted fashionable guests. This was followed a year later by the prestigious *Victoria Hotel*, which was built on the corner of Nevill Street and the Promenade.

A feature of the procession at the opening of the baths was the 50 scholars of Mr. Walker's Academy. This expensive and long-lasting private school was only one of a number of such institutions in Southport. The first evidence of a private school in Southport was as early as 1813.[13] In 1826 Glazebrook provided the details of six private schools in the town, whilst in 1848 Robinson lists twenty-one.[14]

By 1841, there were 1,273 houses in Southport with a population of 7,774. It seems that the landowners gained little from the early development of the town, and appeared to have little interest in it. As late as 1841, Peter Hesketh Fleetwood, who had inherited the estate in 1824, received only £215 per annum in rental from 14 acres of new land which had been leased for building.[15] His major concern was an attempt to develop Fleetwood as a watering place and major ferry port for Ireland and Scotland. Here he spent lavishly on providing sea defences, streets, hotels, houses, public buildings and a railway link to Preston in an ill-fated effort to stimulate development. His ambitious scheme for Fleetwood ran him into disastrous debt. Sir Henry Bold-Hoghton, who had inherited the Bold estate in 1824 through marriage, was also in strained financial circumstances. In an attempt to raise capital, he offered his Southport leaseholders the opportunity to translate to freeholdings for only £40. Fewer than twenty people took advantage of this offer.[16]

During Southport's first 50 years, a combination of a local sea-bathing tradition, the proximity to heavily populated industrial areas, transport links, entrepreneurial initiative, and the acquiescence, if not the active involvement, of the landowners had resulted in it becoming firmly established as a seaside resort.

Notes

1. C. Jacson, *Formby Reminiscences* (1879), p. 93.
2. W. Farrer, *A History of the Parish of North Meols* (1903), p. 62.
3. W.T. Bulpit, *Notes on Southport and District* (1908), p. 75.
4. S. Harrop, *Old Birkdale and Ainsdale: Life on the south-west Lancashire Coast 1600-1851* (1985). This scholarly account also informs the early history of the Township of North Meols.
5. T.K. Glazebrook, *A Guide to South-Port, North Meoles, in the County of Lancaster* (1809), p. 48.
6. E. Hall (ed.), Miss Weeton, *Journal of a Governess 1807-1811* (1936), p. 168.
7. P. Fleetwood-Hesketh, *Murray's Lancashire Architectural Guide* (1955), p. 172.
8. W.M. Ashton, *The Evolution of a Coast-Line: Barrow to Aberystwyth and the Isle of Man* (1920), p. 101.
9. H.J. Perkin, 'The "Social Tone" of Victorian Seaside Resorts' in *Northern History* vol.XI (1976), p. 186.
10. F.A. Bailey, *A History of Southport* (1955), p. 76.
11. T.K. Glazebrook, *A Guide to Southport, North Meols, in the County of Lancaster* (1826), pp. 113-114.
12. B. Nightingale, *Lancashire Nonconformity: the Churches of Southport, Liverpool and the Isle of Man* (1893), p. 27.
13. H.J. Foster, 'Variation in the Provision of Secondary Education in the Nineteenth Century: A Regional Study', PhD thesis, Liverpool University (1988), pp. 154-158.
14. F.W. Robinson, *A Descriptive History of Southport* (1848), p. 73.
15. J. Liddle, 'Estate management and land reform politics: The Hesketh and Scarisbrick families and the making of Southport, 1824 to 1914' in D. Cannadine (ed.), *Patricians, power and politics in nineteenth-century towns* (1982), p. 138.
16. *Ibid.*, p. 138.

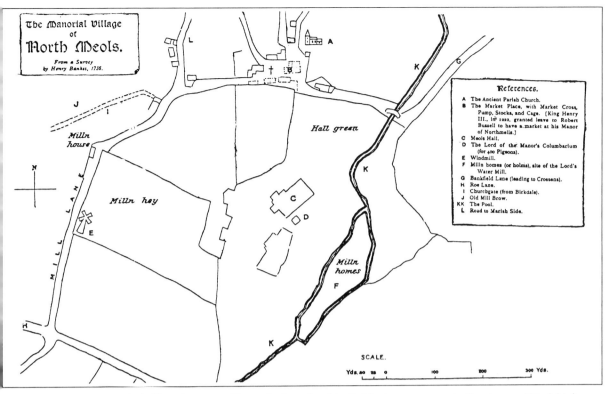

The Manorial Village
of
North Meols.

From a Survey
by Henry Bankes, 1736.

Hall green

Milln
house

Milln hey

Milln
homes

SCALE.

Yds. 50 25 0   100   200   300 Yds.

1 The presence of a windmill and water mill emphasises that North Meols was an agricultural area. 'Marish' is an alternative word for Marsh. After the Hesketh family left Meols Hall in 1733, it was allowed to deteriorate, being sub-divided and tenanted by farmers and later the lord's agent.

2 Behind the Hall were the ruins of the pigeon cote (or Columbarium), which would have been a source of fresh meat in winter.

3 In the centre of this rather romantic 1853 Herdman panorama of Old Churchtown is the *Bold Arms*, and on the other side of the church the *Hesketh Arms*. William 'Duke' Sutton used donkey-carts to transport visitors to the bathing-shelter he had built at South Hawes.

4 Although the North Meols parish church of St Cuthbert's dates back to the middle ages, little of the original fabric survived into the 19th century. This photograph, taken about 1859, shows the church, adjoining cottages and the new iron pump.

5 The doorway of this cottage extended to the eaves and was about four foot seven inches in height. This was '... too low to admit a middle-sized man without stooping.'—J. Binns, *Notes on the Architecture of Lancashire* (1851), p. 34. This was one of a small group of cottages at Westward, between what is now Cambridge Road and Hesketh Road. The older boy was the author's father.

6 Local farms were more substantial than the cottages. For example, these buildings (now nos. 79 and 81 Roe Lane) have a second storey.

7a & b (*above left* and *above*) The cottages were made from local materials. As can be seen in these photographs of Bunting's Farm in Ainsdale, a rough timber 'cruck' frame was secured with wooden pegs, and the wall spaces filled with clamstaff and daub. Charles Weld-Blundell, the squire of Birkdale, described the cottages as 'mud and stick'. The reference is C.J. Weld-Blundell, *What's Wrong with England* (1919), p. 72.

7c (*left*) Thatch was an ideal roofing material, the insulation it provided made the cottages warm in winter and cool in summer. The thickness of the thatch is revealed by the mortar scars on the chimney of a Mill Lane cottage.

8   Belle Vue Cottage was built in 1797. This early marine villa was a refined version of the local cottages. The windows were much larger and included a bay, whilst the stuccoed white painted walls extended above the door before reaching the thatched roof.

9   In 1798 William Sutton built the *South-Port Hotel*. Four years later financial problems forced him to transfer the licence to two Wigan businessmen, although he continued as landlord. Peter Aughton, in his *North Meols and Southport: A History* (1988), effectively demonstrates the ambiguities about the precise form of the inn by comparing illustrations, maps and plans.

10 (*right*) Leigh's 1824 Plan of Southport shows the initial development around Sutton's *South-Port Hotel*, with later linear development north east along Lord Street. A series of cross and parallel roads added a little depth to the hamlet, which was beginning to acquire the facilities of a watering place.

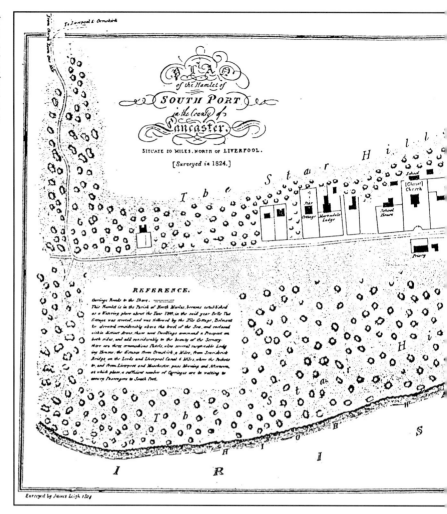

11 (*below*) Herdman's painting demonstrates the manner in which domestic dwellings, on the seaward side of Lord Street, were adapted for use as shops. On the extreme right is the *Scarisbrick Arms*, erected in 1821. This hotel owned more than half of the carriages which daily plied between the canal at Scarisbrick Bridge and the town.

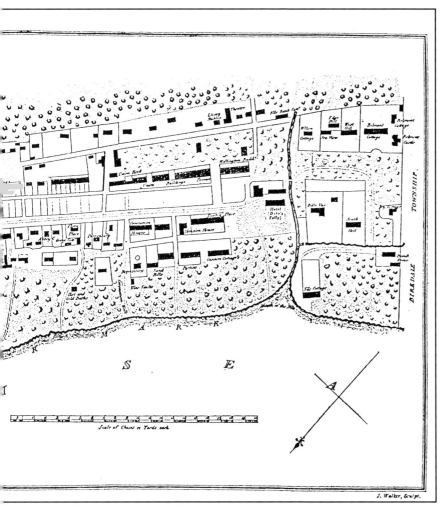

12 (*below*) The *Union Hotel*, was erected in 1805 by 'Duke' Sutton's son-in-law, William Gass. It quickly became the fashionable venue for local meetings and was later to become Southport's premier hotel—*The Prince of Wales.*

13 Christ Church, consecrated in 1821, was a modest brick-built structure. Bank House, beyond the church to the left, was the home of the Rev. William Docker. Like many contemporary vicars he supplemented his income by running an academy for boys. On the right and to the rear of the church was Southport's first 'popular' day school.

14 Herdman's painting shows the rear view of Christ Church and the school. On the left is the Independent Chapel from which Chapel Street took its name.

15 The Promenade, between Coronation Walk and Nevill Street, served the dual purpose of providing a fashionable parade for which pedestrians were charged a toll and, of greater importance to the promoters, it provided sea-front building plots. The building with the classical columns was The Lodge at which tolls were paid and refreshments and novelties were bought.

16 A second company extended the sea-wall north of Nevill Street and built the Victoria Baths. This engraving shows the baths, and the *Victoria Hotel*. The fishermen's small jetty was also used by visitors as a primitive toll pier.

17a & b The homes of some of Southport's wealthy early residents were truly 'castles in the sand'. In 1820, at the south end of the infant town, the extrovert Robert Holt from Wigan built the extravagant castellated Belmont Castle close to the Birkdale boundary whilst magistrate Ralph Peters built View Lodge (later Woodlands) at the northern end of Lord Street. Both buildings subsequently housed schools. Belmont Castle was demolished in 1890, when the lease expired, and Woodlands in 1938.

Chapter Two
New Landowners and a new Era: 1842-1905

The Scarisbricks, a Catholic family, were the major landowners of Southport's agricultural hinterland. Charles (later Sir Charles) Scarisbrick was a younger son whose business energy and determination led to him amassing a considerable personal fortune. By the time of his death in 1860, he was judged to have become '... probably the wealthiest commoner in Lancashire'.[1] It seems that he had been extremely successful in secretive property speculation, possibly including extensive holdings in Paris.[2] Certainly he had money to invest and, having observed the success of emerging Southport, he was determined to extend his influence to include the resort.

The financial problems faced by Peter Hesketh Fleetwood had become more and more acute as his Fleetwood dream turned into a nightmare. It was a 'black hole' swallowing capital, which in turn forced him to consider selling his North Meols estate. Initially he made an agreement to sell to Charles Scarisbrick but, following discussions within the family, he reneged on this undertaking and in 1842 he sold to his younger brother, the Rev. Charles Hesketh, who had been resident in North Meols as rector since 1835.

Charles Scarisbrick was not to be excluded from the growing resort and had also been negotiating with Southport's other landowner, Sir Henry Bold Hoghton. He, too, was heavily in debt and sold his share of North Meols to Scarisbrick for £132,000.[3]

The Rev. Charles Hesketh had paid his brother £148,000 for his share of North Meols, which left him with a heavy burden of mortgage to service. In 1843, Scarisbrick paid him £91,000 for the Hesketh land in the town centre. After this purchase, Scarisbrick owned all of central Southport from the Birkdale boundary to Seabank Road in the north. The remnant of the Hesketh lands stretched further north from the, as yet, undeveloped sandhills of the area which was to become Hesketh Park, across Marshside to Crossens, and inland to Churchtown and what was to become High Park.

Scarisbrick certainly had the resources to indulge his desire to take over Southport. Further evidence of his wealth was his lavish spending on re-building and furnishing Scarisbrick Hall.[4] It appears that his motive for purchasing Southport was to secure the financial future for three illegitimate children born to a former family servant with whom he lived.[5] A trust was set up to provide them with an income from the development of Southport.

When land is concentrated in the hands of one owner he is able to exercise much greater control over the nature of development than is the case when there are many owners. Seaside resorts provide a particularly graphic illustration. Land at Blackpool, Morecambe and New Brighton was in a large number of small holdings, and thus there was an absence of overall control. The 'central area of Blackpool became an ill-planned mass of small properties, boarding houses, small shops, working-class terraces and so on'.[6] In contrast the Clifton family at Lytham and the Scarisbrick and Hesketh families in Southport were able to exercise strict control on development.

Following the haphazard development which had been allowed during the first 50 years, the Scarisbrick estate set a new management pattern in Southport. Driven by the urge to make money, Charles Scarisbrick did not share the active style of landownership which finally bankrupted Peter Hesketh Fleetwood at Fleetwood, but was successful for the landowners of Bournemouth and Eastbourne. Not for him the financing of roads and infra-structure to attract development. The Scarisbrick estate policy was to develop Southport as a socially select middle-class town. It was formulated merely to maximise income. The estate sold leases on large plots for middle-class villas, which were regulated by covenants. These dictated the minimum value for the property to be built and imposed strict conditions relating to building materials to be used and the forming and maintenance of the grounds. The estate waited until leases were sold before the roads were built. Building high-value villas on plots with leases of only 99 years, the estate could look forward to high reversionary values on its land. Many have judged that this estate policy exemplified good town planning practice. It appears that this was just a fortuitous by-product.

The coming of the railways tranformed the town's prospects. The first section of the Liverpool to Southport line opened in 1848, and then, seven years later, came the link with Manchester and inland Lancashire. The '... growing tendency of the upper strata of the commercial world, created and fostered by the general facilities of locomotion, to live away from their business activities' was later identified by a government official as the basis for Southport's rapid growth.[7]

In addition to transport links, middle-class residents desired social exclusiveness, wishing to escape from the industrial environments in which they had made their money. They had also discovered scenery and looked for fine views, and where these did not exist landscape gardeners were able to compensate for nature's shortcomings. The greatest blight in industrial areas was smoke from factories and high-density domestic properties. At Southport, the prevailing south-westerly winds brought clear fresh air, or ozone as Victorians preferred to call it, giving a salubrious climate and enabling the town to score heavily on the health factor. The middle classes also looked to the availability of churches, cultural and social amenities, and a shopping centre.

Southport was able to fulfil the requirements of the potential residents, who came in numbers despite the refusal of the landowner to prime the pump by building the roads or sewering them prior to their arrival. From the beginning, Southport proved to be popular with retired members of the middle classes and particularly with spinsters and widows living from an income. This trend helped to sway the town's population in favour of females.

The resort lacked effective local government. The farmer-dominated North Meols Parish Vestry, operating from Churchtown, had long been responsible for such as there was. The residents of the vigorously growing resort had little in common with the indigenous residents of the remainder of the sparsely-peopled parish. It was the question of street lighting which triggered the agitation which resulted in an Act of Parliament and the setting up of Improvement Commissioners for an administratively separate Southport in 1846. The newly constituted town of Southport extended from the Birkdale boundary in the south to a point about midway across what is now Hesketh Park. Although it was a mile and a half in length it only extended inland to a depth of about half a mile.

The first Commissioners included five clergymen, five gentlemen of independent means, eight substantial traders, and two doctors. Local government was firmly in the hands of a middle-class élite, whose vision for the town was in harmony with the landowners' marketing strategy.

The railways not only allowed middle-class residents to commute to their businesses, with a number of early morning 'First Class' expresses providing an excellent service, they also provided relatively cheap access for visitors. Nathaniel Hawthorne, the American novelist who lived in Southport during the 1850s, described the town as 'seeming to be almost entirely made up of lodging houses'.[8] The 1851 Census showed that only 85 out of the town's 727 houses were lodging houses, whilst further visitors were accommodated in the five hotels and inns. The most dramatic impact made by the railways was, however, their capacity to carry huge numbers of day trippers. In Whit week 1855, the *Southport Visiter* described how 'The railways from the manufacturing district poured in their thousands daily, who flowed through the streets in one vast living stream, and swarmed down the great expanse of shore like a newly-disturbed ant hill'.[9] Over 40,000 came in that week via the Lancashire and Yorkshire and East Lancashire railways alone.[10] Some local residents were not slow to profit from these visitors: fishermen provided boat trips, farmers their donkeys, whilst stalls and side shows waited on the beach at the head of Nevill Street, along which the tide of trippers flooded from the station to the sea, past shops offering them food and fancy goods.

Having left the manufacturing towns to seek social seclusion at the seaside, the middle-class residents had no wish to share their resort with working-class trippers. The threat which trippers were perceived to pose galvanised the estates, the local authority and residents into action. For example, there was a tightening up on the granting of licences for public houses. The Rev. Charles Hesketh, the 'Squarson', influential as Rector and joint Lord of the Manor, led the moral crusade. He was a founder of the town's Total Abstinence Society; he had prohibited race meetings on the sands; and, as a pillar of the Lord's Day Society, he strenuously opposed the running of trains, trading, or any forms of entertainment on a Sunday. Samuel Boothroyd, one of the Improvement Commissioners, who was later regarded as the 'Father of the Council', led the Association to Promote the Improvement and Prosperity of Southport, urging that the town should be advertised 'both as a place of permanent residence and also as a place of resort for invalid visitors'.[11] He argued that Southport prospered because of the '... wise provision made for the accommodation of the religious public by the erection of churches and chapels'.[12] The generosity of Southport's Victorian benefactors transformed the town's skyline. Towers and steeples came to dominate the low-lying landscape. The churches, largely built in stone in Gothic style, appeared as islands of texture and colour contrast in Southport's sea of red brick houses. Indeed, in a speech made by the Mayor—Harold Broderick—in 1913, he claimed that Southport was unique in England as it contained '... more churches and chapels than licensed houses'.[13] The churches were well attended. The census of 1851, the only one ever to include a religious survey, identified Southport as one of the most church-going communities in the country, with 87.8 per cent of the population at church on the census day. A local survey taken 30 years later came up with a similar figure.[14]

Initially it was the Scarisbrick estate which was able to take advantage of the middle-class demand for houses. In 1848, the hiatus over the ownership of Birkdale was finally resolved in the House of Lords, and the new landowner—Thomas Weld-Blundell—immediately sought to share in this market.[15] Southport's west end had come to an artificially abrupt halt at the Birkdale boundary. It was here that Weld-Blundell created a high-class residential suburb of Southport—Birkdale Park.[16] All the conditions necessary for the success of such a suburb were met. Weld-Blundell, who had little capital available after his lengthy legal battle to obtain ownership of Birkdale, followed the marketing strategy of the Scarisbrick estate. Like Scarisbrick this was no high-minded desire to create a model town; it was sound commercial sense on the part of a single landowner. By 1866, a local directory included the following description of Birkdale Park: 'The buildings are generally of a scale of grandeur and magnificence superior to those of Southport, and many are occupied by opulent merchants and manufacturers from Liverpool and Manchester, as well as other wealthy and respectable persons.'[17] The Rev. Charles Hesketh appeared to be missing out on the building boom. There was an empty gap between the northern end of development along Lord Street and Hesketh land. Furthermore Charles Hesketh had a very conservative approach to land ownership. The hard family lesson he had learned in observing his brother's financial ruin in Fleetwood had persuaded him against speculation. A fairy godmother appeared when the Improvement Commissioners were granted additional powers in 1865, including the laying out and maintenance of public parks—an ideal amenity for middle-class residents. The Hesketh hills, particularly Happy Valley, to the north of the town had long been a popular excursion spot. Under their new powers, the Commissioners wanted to buy 30 acres in this area for a public park. Hesketh, who was a Commissioner, refused their offer, but in turn he offered to give the land to the town, subject to a number of conditions. The Commissioners were required to build a wall, provide 'four handsome entrance gates', lay out and maintain the park, and then, most significantly from his point of view, they had to make the road around the park, lay sewers and connect them to the town's sewers, which were still some distance away near the end of Lord Street.[18] At the expense of the ratepayers, land which had been useless sandhills was transformed into valuable building plots, and Hesketh's reputation as a generous benefactor was enhanced.[19] Like Weld-Blundell, he followed the Scarisbrick strategy: a circle of large villas soon ringed Hesketh Park and a new high-class suburb was born.

The other landowners were also aware of the impact a park could have on residential development and both tried unsuccessfully to manipulate their respective authorities. In 1870 the Scarisbrick Trustees offered Southport 15 acres for a park, off Scarisbrick New Road, which was declined;[20] whilst the Weld-Blundells unsuccessfully offered land in Birkdale in both 1875 and 1888.[21]

A contemporary described the residents of the Hesketh Park area as '... professional and mercantile grandees, with a fair sprinkling of snobs, whose position is gauged by the size of the house and the number of servants they kept'.[22] The 1881 census returns show that every house in the Hesketh Park area had at least one resident servant, and only 14 per cent had as few as one; whilst 13 per cent had four or more.[23] In Birkdale Park, 28 per cent of the households had only one servant, whilst 10 per cent had four or more. One of the largest establishments was at Lismore, the Waterloo Road home of the sugar refiner William Macfie, the commander of the Volunteeers, and a leading local politician. He lived there with his wife and six children. In 1891 they were looked after by eight resident servants, including a page. The majority of the servants were female, further swinging the balance between males and females in the town.[24] The architectural style of the houses— Castles in the Sand—reflected the high social tone. Most of them had servants' quarters on an upper floor, with access usually restricted to a rear staircase; and several also had detached quarters, frequently in the form of mews, for outside servants. A letter to the editor of the *Southport Visiter*, in 1888, spoke of 'tasteful gardens, with carefully tended lawns, beautiful trees, with their graceful foliage and refreshingly welcome shade, and the glorious display of exquisite flowers, with every exquisite variation of form, hues and odours, show the great love of beauty in the minds of those who dwell in this favoured region'.[25] It also demonstrated the wealth of the inhabitants who could afford to import the topsoil and manure necessary to render the thin blown-sand fertile, and thus create the garden city at their own expense. In 1888, a feature writer in the *Liverpool Porcupine* speculated that Southport was 'the richest town in the world in proportion to its population', adding that 'more than half of the householders were independent'.[26] A high proportion of these residents, living on income from capital, were female.

The success of the town in attracting residents—by 1891 the population of Southport was 32,191, whilst that in Birkdale was 12,387—resulted in other railway companies running lines into the town. The busy commuter line to Liverpool was electrified in 1904, the first in England to be so developed.[27] 'Southport has had 22 railway stations in its history and for many years 16 were in use simultaneously.'[28] It has been conjectured that this might be a record for a town of its size.[29]

Despite Southport's increased accessibility, the interests of its middle-class residents were not to be served by developing the town as a popular down-market holiday resort. A Park Crescent resident living opposite to Hesketh Park later recalled that: 'The tripper was regarded with high disdain; the town's leaders flew at higher game by trying to draw to Southport the wealthier and more cultured classes.'[30]

The landowners, although reluctant to finance amenities, were willing to provide sites for 'the grand developments' so attractive to the middle classes.[31] The Commissioners took advantage of the great width of Lord Street to make a 'boulevard or public garden' on the east side. Later came the policy of planting trees in the pavements. Following the town's incorporation as a borough in 1867, the Council built the Cambridge Hall, alongside the Town Hall. This provided a first-class venue for meetings and entertainments.

Entrepreneurs invested enthusiastically to provide refined entertainments for both residents and wealthier visitors. In Churchtown, the new Botanical Gardens became a popular excursion venue, as did the menagerie and gardens inland of the town at Kew. The pier (1860) and the replacement Victoria Baths (1871) improved amenities in the town centre, whilst over £90,000 was invested to build the massive Winter Gardens on an eight-acre site between Lord Street and the Promenade. Opened in 1874, it included a conservatory, a concert pavilion, an aquarium and later an opera house. The Glaciarium, at the north end of Lord Street, claimed to be the first such facility in England, and allowed not only skating but also the Caledonian sport of curling to be practised throughout the year. On Lord Street a large first-class hotel—the *Prince of Wales*—replaced the old *Union Hotel*. Shopping, also, was important to the middle classes and a large central shopping area, of regional significance, was developing. The 1891 Census revealed that the town had over 500 lock-up shops.

The entrepreneurs included local politicians who were also involved in the 'moral crusade'. Samuel Boothroyd, the founder of a major Lord Street store, was the principal promoter of the Pier Company. Walter Smith, four times mayor of Southport and an active advocate of temperance, was the Chairman of the Winter Gardens Company, Botanic Gardens Company, the Birkdale Park Land Company, and the Southport and Cheshire Lines Extension Railway Company. It was his rôle as builder of this railway that led to his bankruptcy.

Philanthropy, which gave Southport such an array of churches and chapels, also provided a range of other facilities. For example, John Fernley, a retired Stockport cotton spinner living at Clairville in Birkdale Park, provided a drinking fountain and barometer on the Promenade for the local fishermen, the Meteorological Observatory in Hesketh Park, the land for the Infirmary, and a new lifeboat; whilst William Atkinson, a cotton manufacturer living on the Promenade, was a major contributor to the cost of the Infirmary, and gave the Cambridge Hall clock and the Free Public Library and Art Gallery. The latter two cost him over £13,000 and bore his name.

Stalls and sideshows on the beach were hardly consistent with the emerging vision of the town's future. One contemporary referred in 1877 to 'the exhibition of buffoonery and fairground in the sands near the pier' which he claimed did not 'improve the respectability of the place'.[32] The retreat of the sea allowed the digging of the Marine Lake and the creation of the Marine Gardens fronting the Promenade. These more 'desirable' amenities saw the progressive pushing of the 'popular' amusements south along the lakeside, until they were finally coralled, in 1922, within an enclosed site—'Pleasureland'. 'The Southport fathers, casting a contemptuous glance across the estuary towards Blackpool, said they would never sully the fair expanse of Southport sands with such vulgar aids to amusement as those which disfigure the Blackpool foreshore.'[33]

Southport partly owed its origin to the supposed health-giving properties of sea-bathing and had long been popular as a place of residence and resort. A series of handbooks promoted Southport and Birkdale as health resorts for invalids.[34] The presence of bath-chairs, which stood in rows awaiting hire on Lord Street, testified to the importance of this aspect.

Although not a spa town, Southport developed a range of hydropathic establishments. The *Smedley Hydropathic Hotel*, deep in Birkdale Park, was opened in 1877. It was so successful that Birkdale's massive but financially troubled *Palace Hotel*, which had opened in 1866, was re-organised as a hydro in 1881. Within the town centre Mr. Kenworthy's *The Limes Hydro* in Bath Street offered a range of treatments, whilst at *Rockley House Hydro*, which was situated on the corner of Queen's Road by Hesketh Park, there was later an emphasis on electrical treatments. Victoria Baths also provided a wide range of baths and services. A local directory described it 'as probably the finest and most perfectly appointed bathing establishment of any seaside or other town in England'.[35] It is the business of a directory to be 'congratulatory' and this assessment might have been an exaggeration; nevertheless there were seven plunges, 69 private baths and a number of other specialist treatment baths. The town had its own meteorologist who took readings at the observatory, which was favourably situated high on a hill in Hesketh Park, and daily published figures testifying to the purity of the air and the amount of ozone in the atmosphere. The town's motto '*Salus Populi*' (Health of the People), reflected not only the borough's pride in its general hygienic condition, but also the perceived status of the town as a health resort.

Nevertheless, turning its back on the mass tripper, Southport's holiday trade declined: 'Visitors who came to inhale the ozone-laden breezes were not numerous enough to bring prosperity, and the seekers after refined intellectual pleasure of the kind provided did not discover the charms of Southport in sufficient numbers to do any good.'[36]

One direct outcome was the failure of the Winter Gardens venture. By 1880, Southport was the third largest seaside resort in the country, but after this date it declined relatively as a resort while increasing vastly in importance as a residential town. By the turn of the century, Southport, although the oldest of the Lancashire resorts, was the least dependent on the holiday trade.[37] The provision of homes and services for the wealthy residents and catering for seasonal visitors, provided employment for the majority of the town's population. A government report described Southport in the early 1890s as: 'being intended for pleasure rather than work, it is bright and clean looking with no manufacture and its chief trade is that of building'.[38]

Southport had come to dominate the area; it absorbed Blowick and High Park in 1865, and Churchtown and Crossens 10 years later. One result of the building restrictions imposed by the landowners was a shortage of small cheap houses in and around the town centre.[39] The cheapest property, used by unskilled labourers, was to be found in distant semi-rural Crossens in the north. There, rows of small brick houses joined the scattered thatched cottages. At the turn of the century, the vicar, the eminent local historian the Rev. W. Bulpit, wrote of his parishioners: 'We have no artisans, labourers earn £1 per week with deductions for the loss of time for rain and frost ... people reside in the village for cheapness and walk to town for employment.'[40]

The quickest growing dormitory was High Park, which extended south from Churchtown and was closer to the town than Crossens. 'The houses let mostly at about £10 to £15 per annum and are occupied by the labouring and artisan classes ... labourers, bricksetters, joiners, etc., with few exceptions the remainder are small shopkeepers.'[41]

The normal rate for a joiner was about four pence an hour, giving a wage of about £2 for a 50-hour week, but work was casual, being subject to both demand and the vagaries of the weather. A similar residential pattern to that in Southport could be observed in Birkdale, inland of the railway. The area around Matlock Road was comparable to High Park. In 1883, the vicar of St Peter's wrote: 'The inhabitants are mostly cottagers, who have been compelled to migrate there in consequence of the destruction in Southport of the small dwelling houses in which they formerly resided. Their houses have been pulled down in order to make room for the erection of better classes of houses, and they have found Birkdale habitations suited to their needs.'[42]

Further out from the town centre, the agricultural area of Birkdale Common provided very cheap housing similar to that in Crossens. An interesting feature of the employment statistics was the high incidence of gardeners who produced the fine floral displays which were such a feature of the local villas.

Unlike the authorities in many northern towns and cities, those in Southport and in Birkdale chose not to build municipal houses, and the provision of low cost accommodation was left to the market. By contemporary standards the workers were well housed. 'The labouring class live for the most part in semi-detached pairs of cottages, with back and front gardens.'[43] Terraces were rare in Southport. Moonlight flitting to evade rent or debt, which was a characteristic of other urban areas, was not particularly prevalent in Southport and Birkdale.[44]

The areas between these working-class dormitory estates and the high-class residential property were progressively filled by pairs of semi-detached houses, frequently dubbed 'villas', in which skilled tradesmen, shopkeepers, clerks, minor managers and legions of retired couples, widows and spinsters aped their social betters. They frequently kept a single servant, usually a young girl in her first place. This ensured that the hostess did not have to answer the door to admit visitors. The very act of keeping a servant allowed status-conscious residents to maintain appearances and derive what have been described as 'the psychic benefits'.[45]

As the town expanded, older cottage properties were frequently demolished to accommodate the building of newer higher-value houses. Cottages did survive in numbers in the largely unchanged shrimping, fishing and cockling community of Marshside, and in Churchtown.

A by-product of Southport's development as a socially exclusive residential town was that it became one of the north's chief centres for private boarding schools.[46] The success of the private schools did not rest solely on the influx of boarders; there was a rich reservoir of potential day-pupils. It was locally held that houses with a rental greater than £25 'did not except under peculiar circumstances contain children who use public elementary schools'.[47] In 1867, 40 per cent of Southport's 3,000 houses were in this category. The 1881 Census shows that, in Southport and Birkdale, boarders numbered just under 1,000, of whom some 60 per cent were girls, another contributing factor to the imbalance between the sexes in Southport. The large houses in the town, particularly in the Hesketh Park area, provided suitable premises for private schools and in the 1890s a government commissioner reported: 'Private schools spring up when and where they are wanted through private enterprise; it must be borne in mind that individuals select such localities ... as are pleasant and attractive, and where boarders are likely to come. Thus it is that places such as Southport ... become the happy hunting ground of the private schoolmaster.'[48]

Socially homogeneous Birkdale Park also proved to be an ideal location for private schools. The Commissioner observed that 'Birkdale especially teems with them, there being more brass plates than one could count'. Drawn by the social seclusion and the health factor, private schools were an acceptable 'industry' in keeping with the ethos of the town.

Golf was brought to Southport when a group of middle-class residents formed the Southport Golf Club in 1885. The course was situated in the Hesketh Estate's Marshside Hills.[49] In 1891 the club moved to Scarisbrick land at Moss Lane. The probable reason was the proximity of the course to Little Ireland, an area which a Mayor of Southport had described as 'the main dark spot on the face of the town'.[50]

Little Ireland had sprung up in the 1840s. Isolated amidst the wilderness of Marshside Hills, it was well removed from the town. The inhabitants of this squalid collection of houses gained their living as charwomen, cocklers, donkey drivers and rag and bone gatherers. Over a hundred people lived there amidst a cluster of pigsties, hencotes and stables. It gained itself an unsavoury reputation as a rural slum, infamous for drinking and fighting. Serious assaults and woundings were regular occurrences.

Following the golf club's move to Moss Lane, the Corporation condemned most of the property at Little Ireland under the Public Health Act. Sanitation was virtually non-existent. 'Three or four only of the houses were provided with privies.'[51] Little Ireland also posed a threat to northward residential development from Hesketh Park. Mrs. Hesketh chose to evict most of the tenants and thus 'cleanse' the area. Given the nature of the inhabitants this was a turbulent exercise.

Following Mrs. Hesketh's death, in her nineties, in 1899, she was succeeded by her grandson Charles Bibby (later Bibby Hesketh, then Bibby Fleetwood-Hesketh). Her daughter had married into the prosperous Liverpool shipping family. A young man, Charles energetically addressed the affairs of the estate. He recognised the potential value of a golf course as a factor in re-generating interest in building in the Hesketh Park area and set about restoring the abandoned golf course and building a clubhouse. The *Southport Visiter* commented: 'It is locally understood that the gift of the site of Hesketh Park was the best investment that the previous Lord of the Manor (the late Rev. Charles Hesketh) made, and it is on the cards that the present owner of the Rookery will through his new links, secure the residential development of his property.'[52]

Substantial rebates off golf club fees were available for residents of the Hesketh estate. Seeing their old seaside links revived and a striking new clubhouse dominating the landscape, the Southport Club opted to return and to adopt the name of Hesketh. The boost to the estate was evident in the villas built in the gap between the course and the park.

Birkdale Golf Club, which was founded in 1889, initially played on a nine-hole course in the Bedford Park area, which was a relatively insalubrious area far removed from the homes of the members.[53] The club moved to its present links in 1897. The landowner Charles Weld-Blundell, who had succeeded his father Thomas, initially allowed the club to have the land at a peppercorn rent. This infertile tract lay well beyond the southern limit of housing in Birkdale Park and thus had value only as a rabbit warren. The presence of a golf course, however, had a stimulating effect on residential development. A councillor told the Council that: 'Numbers of people now resident there would not have come to Birkdale but for the golfing facilities.'[54]

The link between golf and middle-class residential development was early established in Southport: 'As each golf course is completed the lots around become automatically the sites of villas.'[55] The message was not lost on Charles Weld-Blundell and he encouraged the development of the Grosvenor, Southport and Ainsdale, Blundell and Hillside golf clubs on his land.[56] It is interesting to note that whilst golf, a middle-class sport which helped to further his residential ambitions, flourished in Birkdale, he positively discouraged football.

Southport did not escape the contemporary agitation relating to land reform.[57] The fact that the landowners had made a fortune by leasing what was formerly common wasteland and marsh, without laying roads, building houses or providing amenities, aroused local feeling. The question of ownership of the foreshore, which gained in importance as the sea retreated, became a focus of this discontent. It soured the relationship between the local authorities and the landowners in both Southport and Birkdale. This was resolved by the turn of the century and the reconciliation involved Charles Scarisbrick, and later his son, serving as Mayors of Southport and both adopting a far more generous attitude to local causes.[58] Similarly, Charles Weld-Blundell accepted the Chairmanship of the Birkdale Council and, acknowledging that it was a long time since he had done anything for Birkdale, he offered to mark the event with the gift of a library, a scheme overtaken by the provision of a Carnegie Library.

Notes

1. F. Bailey, *A History of Southport* (1955), p. 125.
2. J. Liddle, 'Estate management and land reform politics: the Hesketh and Scarisbrick families and the makings of Southport, 1842 to 1914' in D. Cannadine (ed.), *Patricians, power and politics in nineteenth-century towns* (1982), p. 141.
3. *Ibid.*, p. 138.
4. J. Wans, *A Short History of Scarisbrick Hall* (1949), p. 6.
5. Liddle, *op.cit.*, p. 142.
6. H.J. Perkin, 'The "Social Tone" of Victorian Seaside Resorts in the North-West' in *Northern History*, vol.XI (1975), p. 186.
7. Committee of Council on Education, *Annual Report 1873-1874* (1874), p. 81.
8. N. Hawthorne, *English Notebooks*, vol.2 (1883), p. 343.
9. *Southport Visiter* (hereafter *S.V.*), 7 June 1855. Note the idiosyncratic spelling of 'Visiter'.
10. Bailey, *op.cit.*, pp. 158-159.
11. Liddle, *op.cit.*, p. 149.
12. *S.V.*, 15 January 1857.
13. Bailey, *op.cit.*, p. 122.
14. E.D. McNicoll (ed.), *Handbook for Southport, Medical and General* (1883), p. 15.
15. S. Harrop, *Old Birkdale and Ainsdale: Life on the south-west Lancashire coast 1600-1851* (1985), pp. 134-140.
16. H.J. Foster, *New Birkdale: The Growth of a Lancashire Seaside Suburb 1850-1912* (1995), Chapters 2 & 3.
17. P. Mannex & Co., *History, Topography and Directory of Mid-Lancashire* (1866), p. 246.
18. Southport Reference Library, *Minutes of the Park and Town Hall Committee* (1865-1868). These pencil written minutes reveal the cost to the town of the Squire's gift.
19. See for example: McNicoll, *op.cit.*, p. 11.
20. E.G. Twigg, *Southport into Sefton: An account of Local Government in Southport from 1800 to 1974* (1974), p. 6.
21. *S.V.*, 28 January 1876 and 17 July 1888.
22. *Bootle Times*, 26 January 1889.

23. M. Foster, 'Landownership and Residential Differentiation: a Southport case study 1861-1921', a B.A. dissertation, University of Sheffield, (1987), p. 25.

24. H.J. Foster, *op.cit.*, p. 38.

25. *S.V.*, 28 July 1888.

26. Quoted in *Bootle Times*, 13 March 1888.

27. O.S. Nock, *The Lancashire and Yorkshire Railway* (1969), p. 68.

28. C. Greenwood, *Thatch, Towers and Colonnades: the story of architecture in Southport* (1971), p. 20.

29. Bailey, *op.cit.*, p. 211.

30. W.H. Stephenson, *Albert Frederick Stephenson: A Lancashire Newspaper Man* (1937), p. 36.

31. Perkin, *op.cit.*, p. 186.

32. Bailey, *op.cit.*, p. 171.

33. Stephenson, *op.cit.*, p. 37.

34. D.H. McNicoll, *Handbook for Southport: Medical and General* (1859). Anon., *Birkdale, near Southport: an account of its progress as a health resort* (1882). Anon., *Modern city of Health: Southport* (1895).J.V. Wheeler, 'Southport as a Health Resort' in British Association, *Southport: a Handbook* (1903).

35. G. Wright, *Southport a Century Ago* (1992), unpaginated.

36. Stephenson, *op.cit.*, p.37.

37. T.W. Freeman, H.B. Rodgers and R.H. Kinvig, *Lancashire Cheshire and the Isle of Man* (1966), p. 238.

38. *Royal Commission on Secondary Education* (1894-5), vol.VI, p. 349 (hereafter *Bryce*).

39. *Southport Guardian*, 16 May 1888.

40. *National Society Letter Files*, Southport No.4—Crossens National School.

41. *National Society Letter Files*, Southport No.15—High Park National School, 21 May 1889.

42. *S.V.*, 29 April 1883.

43. Southport Reference Library, *Minutes of Southport School Attendance Committee*, 20 March 1889.

44. H.J. Foster, 'The Influence of Socio-Economic, Spatial and Demographic Factors on the Development of Schooling in a Nineteenth Century Residential Town', M.Ed. thesis University of Liverpool (1976), p. 135.

45. G. Anderson, 'The service occupations of nineteenth-century Liverpool' in B.L.Anderson & P.J.M.Stoney (eds.), *Commerce, Industry and Transport: Studies in Economic Change in Merseyside* (1983), p. 91.

46. *Schools' Inquiry Commission* (1868), vol. IX. p.535.

47. *S.V.*, 13 November 1884.

48. *Bryce* (1895), vol.VI, p. 325.

49. K. Hick, *The Hesketh Golf Club 1885-1985* (1985), pp. 8-44.

50. *S.V.*, 20 October 1876.

51. *S.V.*, 31 August 1889.

52. *S.V.*, 8 April 1902.

53. A.J.D. Johnson, *The History of the Royal Birkdale Golf Club* (1988), pp. 9-21.

54. *S.V.*, 7 April 1908.

55. *S.V.*, 8 May 1906.

56. For a detailed analysis of the relationship between land ownership and the development of golf in this area see: H.J. Foster, *Links along the Line* (forthcoming).

57. Liddle, *op.cit.* In addressing the issue of estate management and land reform, this essay makes a major contribution to the understanding of the development of Southport.

58. *Ibid.*, p. 161.

18 When Charles Hesketh was appointed Rector of North Meols in 1835, he came to live in Row (Roe) Lane, at The Rectory, which had been built in 1826. Following his death in 1860, the family stayed in the house, which was re-named The Rookery. They continued to live there until 1919, when the Heskeths returned to Meols Hall, after an absence of nearly two hundred years.

19 When Charles Scarisbrick inherited Scarisbrick Hall, he immediately planned renovations on an ambitious scale. They were started by A.W. Pugin (the Elder), and were later completed by his son. The photograph shows the hall's main entrance. To match the glories of the house's decoration, the gardens were extravagantly furnished. A bronze stag group, in the front garden, had attracted the attention of Prince Albert at a sale. He is reported to have said to a friend: 'How well they would look in front of Windsor Castle.' Charles Scarisbrick overheard the remark and declared: 'They will look just as well in front of Scarisbrick Hall.' The interior of the house, now Scarisbrick Hall School, is rich in plaster work, handprinted wall papers, and carvings, which are protected by preservation orders.

20 Donkey-carts (or shandry) were a popular and traditional mode of transport in Southport. The low-slung carts were pulled by one, two or three donkeys. This 1858 photograph shows a cart standing on Lord Street.

21 The first railway line to Southport was from Liverpool and arrived in 1848, with the station at Portland Street. The Lancashire and Yorkshire Railway opened a line from inland Lancashire in 1855, with its terminus in Chapel Street. As the same company had taken over the Liverpool, Crosby and Southport Railway, they extended this line also into Chapel Street. This view of the station is as it was when originally built.

22 By 1850, the old 'Duke's Folly' was in a dilapidated condition and blocked the end of Lord Street. It was demolished in 1854 and the Improvement Commissioners later marked the site with a memorial light. This lamp in turn was demolished and the commemorative tablet incorporated into a nearby boulevard wall, close to the road sweeper in this 1860 photograph.

23 Southport's magistrates were reluctant to grant new licences. In 1854, that of the demolished 'Duke's Folly' was transferred to the new *Royal Hotel*, on the Promenade. The engraving shows its distinctive square tower, whilst on the beach the attractions of the seaside resort are depicted.

24 In this photograph of the *Royal Hotel* the bathing machines appear to be parked just above the high-water mark.

25 Charles Scarisbrick would not spend money maintaining the deteriorating surface of the Promenade and in 1858 the Improvement Commissioners took over responsibility and abolished the toll-fee. The surface of the Promenade was improved and building continued. An 1876 photograph shows a continuous line of buildings. The square building on the left is Claremont House, the home of William Atkinson, which now forms part of the British Legion's Byng House.

26 The ferocity of winter storms occasionally played havoc with the fabric of the Promenade. This damage, opposite Bold Street, occurred in 1858.

27 A joint stock company built an iron pier, which was opened in 1860. The photograph of the ceremony includes Fernley's fountain and barometer for local fishermen and a fishing boat alongside the Promenade.

28 Initially 1,200 yards long, the pier was level with the Promenade. The pier-head was a platform, some forty yards long, from which two iron staircases led down onto the beach.

29 By 1868 the pier had been extended to 1,460 yards and a substantial new pier-head accommodated steamers which, at different times, provided services linking Southport to ports from Anglesey in the south to Barrow in the north. Silting of channels later made the approach to the pier impossible. The last steamer sailed in 1923 and the fishing boats were dispersed along the coast.

30 From low-lying Lord Street, excursionists faced an uphill walk along Nevill Street to the raised Promenade. Access to the beach was through a subway and under an iron bridge on the Promenade. As they emerged, alongside the pier, there were entertainments, stalls and donkey rides. This was an area that the town's fathers were anxious to 'tidy up'.

SOUTHPORT.

31 When the landowners sold their rights to the foreshore to the Council, they insisted on the condition that the land in front of the Promenade could only be used for recreation. This opened the way for the digging of the Marine Lake and the laying out of Marine Gardens, on land left by the retreating sea.

32 The South Marine Lake was opened in 1887. Between the gardens and the lake there was an area of sand, where a shallow paddling pool was excavated for the children. The fairgound stalls and entertainments had been moved from alongside the pier to the south end of the lake.

33a, b & c (*above and facing page*) The towers were at the ends of an aerial-ride built to carry passengers across the lake. Promenade residents objected to it as an eyesore and it was removed in 1911. Other attractions included a water chute, which was built in 1903. Many of the attendants were local fishermen.

34a & b Alongside the Water Chute was a flying-machine, designed by Hiram Maxim, the inventor of the machine gun which bore his name. After the removal of the aerial-ride, a miniature railway was built alongside the lake. The beautifully engineered coal-fired steam engines long proved to be a source of fascination.

35 The major rides were joined by increasing numbers of stalls and attractions. In the background can be seen the Winter Gardens. Opened in 1874, it dominated the south Promenade.

36 This photograph shows the Concert Pavilion on the left. It was capable of seating 2,000 people and was to survive until 1962 as a cinema and a theatre. On the right was the Conservatory, which, it was claimed, was the largest in England. Later used as a ball-room and for roller skating, it was demolished in 1933. Under the covered promenade which linked the two principal buildings was a large aquarium. The structure on the left was a stage on which pierrots performed for open-air audiences.

37 (*above*) The Winter Gardens Opera House was added in 1891 and destroyed by fire in 1929. It was replaced three years later by the Garrick Theatre. Beyond the Opera House was the Lord Street station of the Southport and Cheshire Lines Extension Railway. Directors of the Winter Gardens were involved in promoting this railway, which they hoped would bring much-needed visitors to the complex. On the right was a ticket office and entrance to the Winter Gardens.

38 (*right*) Sand yachts had featured on Southport beach from as early as 1842 but were banned following a collision with a bathing-machine. Re-introduced about 1852, Hawthorne described these extraordinary vehicles as '... great clumsy boats on wheels'.

39 (*above*) The North Lake was dug in 1892 and yachts sailed where sand yachts formerly trundled. The running of the boating on the lake was leased to local fishermen. Further Marine Gardens, including a bandstand, were built between the lake and the Promenade. On top of the boathouse was a windmill which powered a pump to raise sea-water for sewer-flushing and street-cleaning.

40 The retaining wall which formed the northern boundary of the lake is still visible as a curved finger reaching out into the enlarged lake. It now serves as a perch for sea birds.

41 As the sea retreated from Southport, a Marine Drive was built in 1894. It enclosed a large area of beach, beyond the lake, which became known as the Lagoon.

42a   The pier looks in very bad shape, its legs had been undermined and the decking had collapsed. The cause was the building of the Marine Drive. A high tide washed over the Marine Drive and filled the Lagoon and the only way in which the water could later escape was through a single outlet. The pressure would have been enormous and the water scoured a deep channel across the beach and under the pier.

42b   The depth of the channel is illustrated by the man standing within it.

42c   The outflow from the Lagoon which caused the pier to collapse.

43 The Marine Drive was an attempt to follow the retreating sea. Many trippers settled for a day at the lakeside.

44 To compensate for the absence of the sea an open-air pool was opened, alongside the Marine Drive, in 1914.

45 An end of the Promenade bridge over the Nevill Street subway is clearly visible. The steps in the centre of the photograph gave access to the subway.

46 The Pier Pavilion was burned down in 1897 and this 1902 replacement, with its minarets, was an excellent example of the genre.

47 Nevill Street was on the direct route from Chapel Street Station to the beach.

48 An alternative route was through Scarisbrick Avenue. The link roads between Lord Street and the Promenade are still dominated by amusement arcades and cafes, where bright façades merely emphasise the undistinguished nature of the buildings.

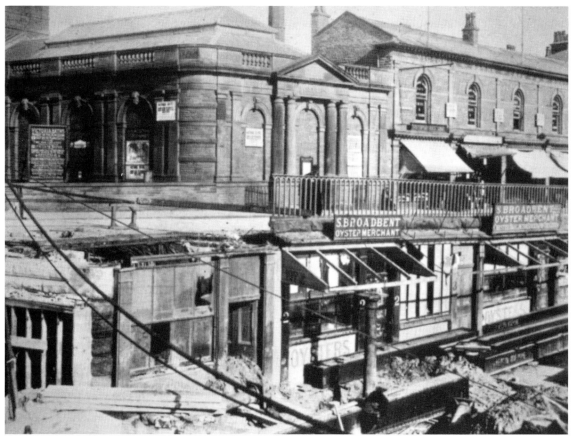

49a & b In 1903 the subway was filled in. The shops on the two levels are clearly visible. Nevill Street was transformed into a broad open approach to the Promenade.

50 The magistrates restricted the granting of drinking licences in the town. One long established 'watering hole', just off Nevill Street, was the *Old Ship Inn*.

51 There were many cafes competing for the excursionists' patronage. Immediately alongside the station in Chapel Street was Hayes' Restaurant, which claimed to be 'The oldest establishment in the town' and offered 'Special terms for picnic parties'. Here the waitresses posed for the camera.

52 The Town Hall was occupied in 1854; the design was both simple and classic. As well as serving the Commissioners, it also provided accommodation for the magistrates, the police and the post office. The gun was a Crimean War trophy, marking the generosity of the residents to the fund for soldiers' widows and orphans.

53 The Commissioners decided on the erection of a municipal hall for meetings and entertainments. It took its name from Princess Mary of Cambridge, who opened it in 1874. The presence of the adjacent houses—Richmond Hill—demonstrates how domestic dwellings had to be demolished in order to accommodate new civic buildings. The Commissioners had set up a Boulevard Committee, in 1864, to undertake the landscaping of Lord Street and the gardens reflect its work.

54 In 1878, a Free Public Library and Art Gallery, which together cost almost £14,000, were given by William Atkinson, who also paid for the installation of a clock and chimes in the Cambridge Hall's lofty tower. The spire of Christ Church can be seen in the background. In 1862, Atkinson had paid for a new stone west front, tower and steeple.

55 The crowded hanging of pictures, in the art gallery, reflected Victorian taste.

56 Frampton's statue to commemorate Queen Victoria was unveiled in the gardens, outside the Art Gallery, on 15 July 1904 by the Mayor, Councillor Brown.

57 In 1877, the gardens in front of the municipal buildings were modified to include a terracotta fountain and an octagonal bandstand.

58 Lord Street continued to be the important shopping street for residents. This photograph was taken about 1860 and shows the area north of the *Scarisbrick Arms*, before tree planting at the edge of the pavement was fashionable, although glass verandahs were already in evidence.

59 The 1870 photograph shows that many of the shops still sold everyday items. They included butchers, grocers and hardware merchants.

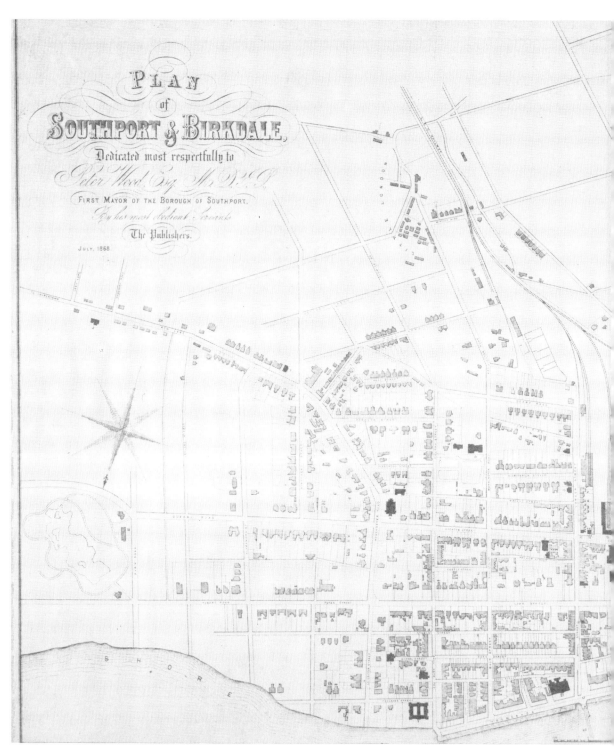

60 Johnson and Green Street Plan, 1868. This accurate street plan shows the consolidation that had taken place in the town centre and the arc of outward expansion.

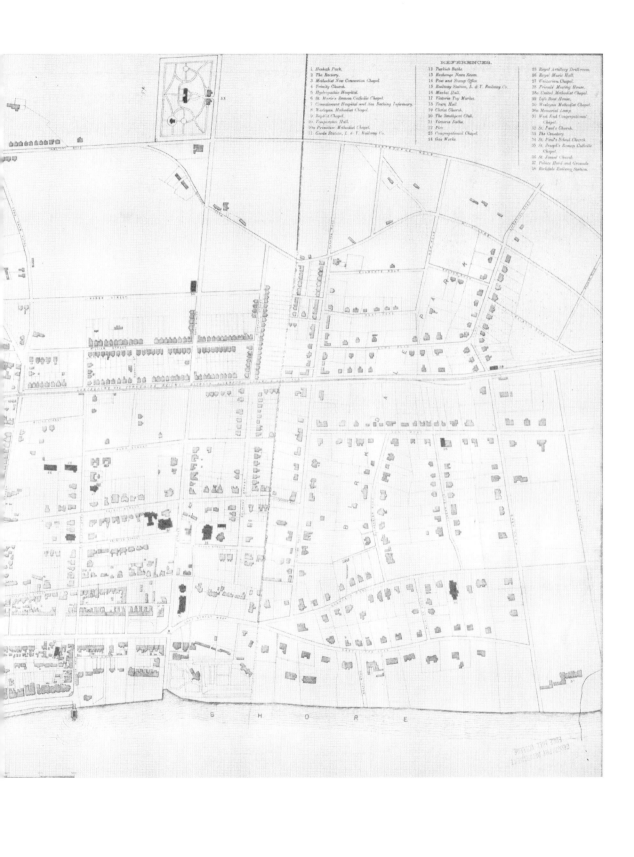

61 Philanthropy provided local churches in extraordinary numbers. For example, Holy Trinity was re-built at a cost approaching £50,000 in the early years of the 20th century. Pevsner described it as 'a tour-de-force of Edwardian patronage'. The nave, west front and tower (which for many years was Southport's tallest building) were given by the Elders, owners of a Liverpool shipping line, whilst the chancel came from donations by Joseph Mallineaux and Joseph Dewhurst, both cotton manufacturers.

62 Under the enthusiastic and generous leadership of Dr. Peter Wood, Southport's first Mayor, the Wesleyans commenced building their mother church in Mornington Road in 1859. The 130-ft. high spire was claimed to be the first in Methodism.

63 Within twenty-five years of the opening of Mornington Road Church it had no fewer than nine daughter churches in the town, although the landowners did not allow the building of Nonconformist churches in the most prestigious residential areas. The £10,000 cost of Trinity Church in Duke Street, which was built in 1863, was borne by John Fernley. John Ruskin judged it to be the finest example of Early English style in the north of England.

St. Maries Church
Southport. 215

64 Catholics were never numerous in Southport and St Marie's on the Sands was built in 1841 in Seabank Road on the northen edge of the developing town. The small aisleless church was designed by the elder Pugin, who had been engaged by Charles Scarisbrick to rebuild Scarisbrick Hall. Major alterations and enlargements, in 1874, removed most traces of Pugin's work.

65 Sir William Hartley, the jam manufacturer, was a major benefactor of Church Street Church, which was built in 1905 at a cost of £25,000. This well-proportioned church was described as the Cathedral of Primitive Methodism, whilst locals dubbed it The Jam Chapel.

66 Churches for minority denominations were much in evidence in Southport. For example, Timothy Coop, a clothing manufacturer from Wigan, came to live in Mornington Road and in 1875 built the Church of Christ in Mornington Road. The building now serves as a judo hall.

67 The re-built Belle Vue was the home of Sir George Pilkington, a mayor of Southport and its first Member of Parliament. He lived there from about 1886 to his death in 1916. It was later to become a hotel and was demolished in 1962.

68 Thomas Weld-Blundell, the new landowner in Birkdale, chose to market his land for development as a high-class residential suburb of Southport—Birkdale Park. One of the first houses—Birkdale Lodge—was built by John Aughton in Lulworth Road in 1850.

69a & b The photographs show the dining room and the billiard room of Birkdale Lodge in 1914.

70 Belair in Trafalgar Road was an example of the great villas which were later built in this area.

71 The opulent entrance hall of Scarisbrick House in Southport. This was built by landowner Charles Scarisbrick's son.

72 The site for Hesketh Park was given to the town by the Rev. Charles Hesketh. This photograph of the opening ceremony in 1859 shows the lodge at the corner of Park Road and Park Crescent. The previously barren nature of the area is evident from the tall sandhills being used as grandstands.

73 This 1869 photograph illustrates how effective the park was in attracting villa development to the Hesketh Estate.

74 All Saints' Church was erected at the corner of Park Road and Queens Road, opposite to the park lodge, in 1871. Many landowners built churches where they were trying to develop high-class residential estates, believing that this would help stimulate growth.

75 Hesketh Park is just visible in the top left-hand corner of this 1930s aerial photograph. The uniformly superior nature of the villas of this residential district is immediately apparent.

76 Park Grange on Park Crescent was the home of Sir Albert Frederick Stephenson, the proprietor of the *Southport Visiter*. Stephenson was a leader of the consortium which bought the Hesketh Estate from Robert Bibby Fleetwood-Hesketh in 1927.

77 Garswood was another of the Park Crescent villas. A feature of these 'castles in the sands' was their conservatories.

78 Hesketh Golf Club provided an example of the beneficial effect of a golf course on villa development in an area. Each of the houses in Hesketh Road had a gate at the bottom of the garden giving access to the course. The central area of the photograph was the site of Little Ireland, the buildings around the car park being remnants of this settlement.

79 Little Ireland was a squatter settlement of people, mainly of Irish extraction, living metaphorically and physically on the fringe of society. It had sprung up in the 1840s when it was well outside the town. With the development of the Hesketh Park area and the golf club it became a socially unacceptable neighbour and the Little Irelanders were evicted.

80a & b Although not a spa, there were a number of hydropathic institutions in the town. In Birkdale Park, the *Smedley Hydropathic Hotel* (*above*), opened in 1877, was an immediate success. The massive *Palace Hotel* (*below*), which had been built in 1866, was not a commercial success and following financial failure was reconstructed as a Hydro in 1881.

80c & d   In Southport *The Limes Hydro* (*above*) was opened by Mr. Kenworthy in 1876. *Rockley House* (later *Hesketh Park*) *Hydro* (*below*), on the corner of Park Road and Albert Road, specialised in electrical treatments.

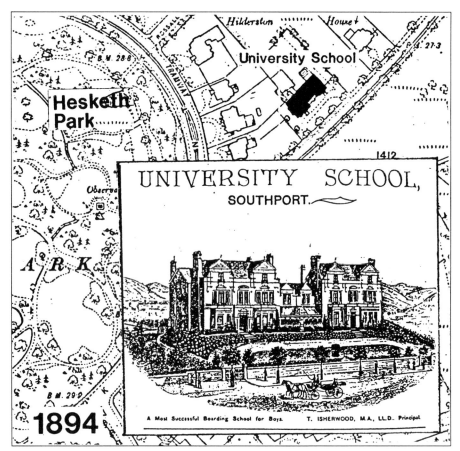

81 One of the largest and most successful of the boys' private schools in the Hesketh Park district was the University School. In 1884, Dr. Thomas Isherwood purchased the first new house to be built in Cambridge Road. Buildings of this type afforded accommodation for substantial schools with facilities for boarders.

82 Like many of the school principals, Isherwood was a substantial figure in the community, serving as Mayor. The 1894 photograph shows him with the school cycling club.

83 Birkdale Park had a number of girls' boarding schools. Hannah Wallis, a Quaker widow, opened a school in Albert Road in 1861 and later transferred to a larger house in Waterloo Road, where she ran Brighthelmston.

84 The Misses Horner took over the premises in Albert Road and their Saxenholme School was attended by generations of local girls and boarders. Both of these successful and long-lasting schools have been victims of the contraction in private school education.

85 Carriages, privately owned or hired, allowed residents and visitors to enjoy the fashionable drive along Lord Street. At the turn of the century bicycles were expensive and much favoured by the middle class. Most of Lord Street's shops had a cycle stand.

86 There were several stands for carriages on Lord Street. This one was on the corner of Eastbank Street. The West Lancashire Bank, in the background, was opened in 1879, and later absorbed into the Atkinson Library.

87 London Square, now the Monument Square, was at the hub of the town's tramway system. The building on the island in the centre of the road was a shelter for cab drivers. In the foreground is a bathchair.

88 A Shakespeare Street supplier and repairer of bath chairs. A contemporary recalled that they were '... popular not only with the infirm, but also with the leisured well-to-do, who largely used this method of conveyance on their shopping expeditions'.

89a A tram is seen approaching London Square.

89b Lord Street was low-lying and subject to flooding. The problem was exacerbated when rain storms coincided with high tides and the water was unable to escape through the outflows on the beach.

90a & b Parades were a popular means of celebrating national and local events. One photograph shows a fire engine passing the *Prince of Wales' Hotel* on Lord Street, and the other the lifeboat *Mary Anna* in Eastbank Street.

91a The suburbs of Southport were served by an unusually large number of railway lines and stations. Birkdale Palace station, Southport and Cheshire Lines Extension Railway.

91b Ainsdale station, Lancashire and Yorkshire Railway.

91c Blowick station, Lancashire and Yorkshire Railway.

91d Churchtown station, West Lancashire Railway.

92a & b In Southport, the cheapest housing was to be found in outlying Crossens, High Park, and Blowick. The street scene is of Rufford Road, Crossens, whilst the aerial view of Blowick shows rows of small semi-detached houses spreading out towards the gas works. It was only in the inter-war years that the local authority addressed Southport's chronic lack of cheap housing and built council houses.

93a & b In Birkdale, as in Southport, cheap housing was confined to the outlying districts. These photographs show the inland end of Kew Road (*above*) and a shop at the corner of Kew Road and Boundary (Guilford) Road (*below*).

94 (*above*) The off-licence at the corner of Upper Aughton Road and Elm Road, Birkdale. The base of the chimney of the Crown Brewery is visible above the corner of the shop.

95 Until amalgamation with Southport in 1912, Birkdale was a separate local authority, with its own council. The photograph shows the municipal buildings which were a symbol of its independence.

96 (*left*) Birkdale developed a town-centre, in Liverpool Road, during the early years of the 20th century. The photograph, looking seaward from Bolton Road, shows how houses and front gardens had to be sacrificed in order to create shops and broad pavements.

97a & b Detached from Birkdale, Ainsdale was an independent township and part of a separate parish. Charles Weld-Blundell unsuccessfully attempted to create a high-class residential area—Ainsdale on Sea—centred on Shore Road (*above*). Long rejected by Birkdale, Ainsdale became a pawn in the amalgamation battle between Southport and Birkdale, and in 1903 it was absorbed by the latter. The photograph below shows the shopping area of Station Road, inland of the railway.

98 The newspaper hoardings, on the photograph of the Botanic Road newsagent, clearly date it as 1914. The Ribble Bus Company time-table is fastened to the wall.

99 Visits to the old village of Churchtown were a popular outing. The Botanic Gardens, with its lake, conservatory and museum was a considerable attraction.

100a & b Between the high-class residential suburbs of Birkdale Park, Hesketh Park and the town centre, there was a collar of substantial detached and semi-detached villa-type properties. Norwood Avenue (*above*) and Sussex Road (*below*) provide examples. Southport's policy of pavement tree-planting extended to the suburbs.

101 The corner of Cambridge Road where new development, encouraged by the tramway and the railway, meets the traditional cottages of the fishing community of Marshside.

102 The growth of the suburbs created a demand for neighbourhood shops, public houses and churches, as evidenced in this photograph of Manchester Road.

103 Scarisbrick New Road ran inland of the town centre. This photograph, from the base of Eastbank Street Bridge, shows an edge-of-town cab shelter, The Baptist Tabernacle, and, in the distance, the tower of St Philip's Church.

104 The Scarisbrick New Road Area was the location of a number of large private schools, which were cheaper than those of Birkdale Park and Hesketh Park. A government commissioner described the education they offered as suitable for the lower middle classes. Respectability was a keynote, as demonstrated by the turn out of the boys at Captain J.C. Underwood's Southport Modern School, on the corner of Scarisbrick New Road and Cumberland Road. The school was popular and had 172 pupils in 1902.

105 In 1892, the local fishing fleet, which operated from the pier head, consisted of about ninety boats manned by nearly four hundred fishermen. Although Marshside is perhaps the best known of the local fishing communities, there was another substantial colony in the St Luke's area. The boats were mainly 'Lancashire Nobbys', which were shallow draught, decked boats with a cockpit.

106 The photograph shows a pair of Marshside fishermen sitting on their 'leaps', whilst waiting for a tram on Lord Street. The 'leap' was a willow basket in which they carried their catch.

107a Most of the boats in the local fishing fleet were built at Marshside and Crossens. Wignall Bros. of Shellfield Road were well-established sailmakers.

107b Outside the sail loft, there was a rope-walk and in the yard was a mast on which sails could be trimmed.

108 Boats were used for fishing and shrimping. Following the dispersal of the fleet, 'shanking' for shrimps was mainly confined to horse-drawn carts.

109 Shrimping was also undertaken on foot using a push net. Hand shrimpers, or 'putters', used a net with a six- or seven-foot beam. The contents of the net were riddled and the shrimps tipped into a 'leap', carried on the 'putter's' back.

110 (*right*) The photograph shows Marshside fishermen parading to the law court in 1913. The procession was led by members of the Marshside Temperance Band. The fishermen had been summoned because of an act of vandalism against a 'badger', who was importing Dutch shrimps and selling them as 'Southport Potted Shrimps'. The fishermen, who produced 'Potted Southport Shrimps', took direct action to defend their livelihood.

111 (*below*) This fisherman's cottage is believed to be at Westward. There is a 'putter's' net and 'leap' against the wall and a net drying on the fence.

112 (*below*) The West Lancashire Railway, with its station at the end of Marshside Road, was used to take some of the catch to market. The post card shows 'Southport fishwives at Preston Market'.

113 The low-lying extensively farmed land of south-west Lancashire did not support a hunt. The gentry's sport was shooting. This early photograph shows a Mr. Tomlinson who was a local gamekeeper.

114 The cow outside the *Bold Arms* is a reminder that the 'Out District', around urban Southport, was still agricultural.

15 There were a number of wheelwrights and blacksmiths in the agricultural districts. Churchtown smithy (pictured) in Botanic Road still survives.

16 There were three windmills in North Meols—Churchtown, Birkdale and Ainsdale (pictured). Although no longer a windmill, milling continued at Ainsdale until relatively modern times.

117 The photograph shows a steam engine driving a threshing-machine at a Crossens farm. In 1875, three boys from St James' School in Birkdale lost their attendance marks through loitering on their way to school in order to watch a couple of steam threshing-machines.

118 Birkdale was the principal agricultural area. In 1851, 80 per cent of the male heads of household were involved in farming. The photograph shows Underhill Farm, near Windy Harbour Road. Here several generations of Rimmers, followed by the Berrys, grew vegetables for local sale and had pasture for about sixteen cows. They sold milk as far afield as the Southport boundary using a horse-drawn milk float. In 1897 there were 157 cows in Birkdale producing 600 gallons of milk daily.

Chapter Three
Southport County Borough: The Seaside Garden City

Southport finally attained County Borough status in 1905. Birkdale, although a suburb of Southport, was still an independent township with its own local authority. The Birkdale Council's policy was to keep expenditure to a minimum and thus set a lower rate than that in Southport, and to do nothing which would disturb the tranquillity of the wealthy ratepayers of Birkdale Park.

Southport coveted the rateable value of the Birkdale properties and had long sought amalgamation. Birkdale had consistently resisted its neighbour's overtures, but finally, in 1912, the cost of finding a solution to its long standing sewerage problems left Birkdale, which had earlier absorbed Ainsdale, with no alternative to accepting Southport's terms.[1] Southport had grown to subsume virtually all of the parish of North Meols.

Becoming a County Borough immediately increased the powers of the local authority, as did a succession of later Parliamentary Acts. Southport was one of the first places to adopt the Town Planning Act of 1909. A committee was established which set about the task of continuing the development of the seaside garden city. One of the committee's earliest acts was to forestall a plan by Charles Weld-Blundell to build a 'garden village' of a hundred bungalows on Birkdale foreshore.[2] Indeed, Southport was able to complete its acquisition of all the Borough's foreshore, and much of the adjacent sandhills, thus preserving open spaces which now contain major national, regional and local nature reserves.

As the landowners sold off their assets, the Council stepped in to buy the Birkdale, Hesketh, and Hillside golf courses. Southport was still attempting to develop itself as a superior residential resort and the Council believed that golf could help promote this image of the town. In 1931, the Birkdale Club agreed to accept a 99-year lease from the Council, in return for the guarantee that the club would re-model the course and build a new clubhouse, in order that major tournaments could be attracted.[3] Royal Birkdale joined Southport and Ainsdale as a host for the Ryder Cup and regularly stages the Open Championship. There were four championship courses within the Borough. In an attempt to support the image of the garden city, Southport Flower Show, which grew to become a national event, was first staged by the Corporation in 1924. Further open space was secured with the purchase of the Botanic Gardens, with generous aid from Roger Fleetwood Hesketh, the son of Charles Bibby Fleetwood Hesketh.

A feature of the 20th century has been the manner in which the three landowners sold off their holdings in Southport. Charles Bibby Fleetwood Hesketh sold virtually the whole Hesketh estate to a property syndicate in 1927. Surprisingly this sale included several hundred acres of prime building land to the north of the town.[4] Excluded was Meols Hall, which had been finally re-occupied by the family in 1921. Roger Fleetwood-Hesketh, who became squire following his father's death in 1947, re-purchased agricultural land and cottages close to Meols Hall. Although no longer a major landowner in Southport, he developed close ties with the community. He served the town as both mayor and M.P. and energetically supported voluntary and charitable organisations. Meols Hall, a modest house, was extensively re-built and he was ever ready to allow its use for worthy causes. Not surprisingly he became a highly respected figure, who was able to live out the rôle of benevolent local squire. The male line of the Weld-Blundell family died out, and the Birkdale estate also was eventually sold.

After years in which it had been run by Trustees, the Scarisbrick estate, which had sold virtually all its town centre building land, was partitioned between the three beneficiaries in 1925. One share was sold off immediately, another in the 1950s, and the final portion in 1978.[5] For residents, obtaining planning permission from the Council became far more significant than restrictions imposed by landowners, particularly as more people bought their freeholds.

One problem facing the planners has been the fate of the 'Castles in the Sand'. The largest Victorian houses are seldom suitable for occupation by single families. Private schools, which formerly used many of them, have found survival difficult. More recently the increased demand for nursing-home places has found a use for many. There are currently 94 such institutions in Southport. The 1991 census figures reveal that Southport has a high proportion of elderly people who live in 'communal establishments'. The figure is 4.3 per cent against a national figure of 1.5 per cent. Given the size of the plots and the height and extent of the old 'castles', developers have been able to build blocks of eight flats on modest sites, and many more on sites such as the four-acre plot on which The Warren stood in Westcliffe Road. After a rash of such developments transformed the appearance of Birkdale Park and the Hesketh Park area, planning permission to replace the old 'castles' appears to be becoming more difficult to obtain.

Southport continued to be the favoured location to which many inland Lancashire residents chose to retire. During the inter-war years, many modest semi-detached houses were built for this market. New arterial roads to the south—Waterloo Road—and to the north—Preston New Road—helped open up the Hillside and Churchtown areas for such development. In 1928, the Southport Council launched a joint marketing campaign with the new owners of the Ince-Blundell and Hesketh estates. More recently this market has been met by the blocks of flats, which have been built to replace older properties nearer to the town centre. The area now has one of the highest older persons population in the United Kingdom.[6]

It was in the inter-war years that the Corporation finally provided rented housing for the working classes. Estates were built on the outer fringes of the town.[7] By 1939 there were 14 such estates with almost 1,000 council houses. The work formerly generated by providing services for the wealthy has shrunk. From the turn of the century, the Vulcan Motor Company had established a modest industrial base in Crossens. Subsequently the growth of light engineering, plastics, textiles, food and drink production resulted in manufacturing becoming the largest employer of labour in Southport.[8] These manufacturers are mostly small units, and the premises are scattered unobtrusively behind the town. Many are on back plots, behind the building lines.

The decline of Liverpool as a shipping and commercial centre and the loss of industrial capacity in the North West has dramatically cut the number of commuters from Southport, but the town has continued to enjoy its position as a regional shopping centre. The advent of retail multiples and the decline in the number of specialist luxury goods shops has eroded some of its distinctive character. The growth of out-of-town shopping poses a threat, but the verandah-covered parade of Lord Street with its attractive arcades still presents a shopping environment different from the air-conditioned uniformity of modern shopping malls.

During the 20th century, the town has continued to struggle to find an identity. Although still a geographical entity, local government re-organisation in 1974 placed it within the Metropolitan Borough of Sefton, an administrative collection of disparate communities. In terms of population the town appears to be static. By 1941 it was estimated to be 85,023; 50 years later the census showed a small fall of 449. The great growth days of Southport appear to be well in the past; nevertheless, building on its environmentally-rich inheritance, the town still proves attractive to residents and those, much reduced in number, who choose to visit it.[9] It remains a shopping centre of distinction. In relation to golf it has rightly been described as a 'mecca': Sefton boasts no fewer than six championship courses. The area is also becoming increasingly important for the presence of major nature reserves.

Notes

1. J.E. Jarratt, *Municipal Recollection: Southport 1900-1930* (1932), pp. 32-42.
2. H.J. Foster, *New Birkdale: The Growth of a Lancashire Seaside Suburb 1850-1912* (1995), Chapter 8.
3. A.J.D. Johnson, *The History of the Royal Birkdale Golf Club: 1889-1989* (1988), p. 32.
4. J. Liddle, 'Estate Management and Land Reform Politics: the Hesketh and Scarisbrick families and the making of Southport 1842 to 1914' in D. Cannadine (ed.), *Patricians, power and politics in nineteenth-century towns* (1982), p. 164.
5. *Ibid.*, p. 166.
6. *S.V.*, 4 November 1994.
7. R.E. Perrins (ed.), *Local Government Exhibition Brochure* (1946), p. 21.
8. T.W. Freeman, H.B. Rogers and R.H. Kinvig, *Lancashire, Cheshire and the Isle of Man* (1966), p. 239.
9. C. Greenwood, *Thatch, Towers and Colonnades: The story of architecture in Southport* (1971). A sensitive, well informed appraisal of Southport's architectural heritage.

119a & b Lord Street, with its canopy of trees on the 'boulevard side' and broad verandah covered pavement on the 'shop side', was Lancashire's most fashionable thoroughfare. The coming of the internal combustion engine introduced motor-driven cycles on the Noonday Parade.

120   Albert Stephenson, of Park Grange, bought this 20 horse-power open tourer Panhard in 1906. When his wife later accepted a closed car, it replaced their carriages.

121   Richard Bamber, at the wheel of his motor car, which is said to be the second in Southport, was a Kensington Road cycle manufacturer who progressed to making motor cycles. Later, as the town's love affair with the motor car developed, he became the premier agent, with prestigious showrooms on Liverpool Road and Lord Street.

122 The quality of the shop buildings extended above the verandahs and these upper stories provided fashionable apartments. There has been little change in this 'shopscape' since the photograph was taken about 1902, although the 'Moorish' cupola was removed before the First World War.

123 Some of the most im-
pressive buildings on Lord
Street were the banks. Cedric
Greenwood, in his *Thatch,
Towers and Colonnades*, judges
Lord Street's Midland Bank to
be Southport's most mag-
nificent building. The vaulted
ceiling of the banking hall
is supported by marble
Corinthian columns, the floor
was mosaic and all the detail
of the highest quality.

124 Floored with marble, finished in mahogany, the Leyland (now Wayfarers') Arcade, off Lord Street, provided an elegant shopping promenade on two levels.

125 The Royal Arcade (now Highton's) was then in multiple occupation. The buildings provide good examples of Lord Street's verandahs.

126 By 1902, the 'multiples', in the shape of Boots Cash Chemists, had arrived on Lord Street, just north of Nevill Street. The photograph includes one of Southport's ubiquitous bathchairs.

127 A vanished facet of Southport's luxury trade was based on the fashionable contemporary aspiration of ladies to have fur coats. The 1924 Seed's Directory listed as many as thirty furriers in Southport. Changed attitudes have seen the extinction of this species. The salon door led to the cold room where customers could store their garments. Master furriers, such as Fletcher's, employed a number of cutters, machinists and finishers who made and re-modelled garments on the premises.

128 Walter Connard opened his jewellery business on Lord Street as early as 1883. The contemporary photograph shows the interior, with echoes of Aladdin's cave. The showcases, minus the Victorian fretwork on the tops, can still be seen in this old family business, which exemplified Lord Street's commitment to quality shopping.

129 The Wayfarers' Shop, another family business, opened by Vyvian Pedlar in 1925, provided shoppers with interior furnishings in the latest English and continental fashions. This corner of a showroom reflected the taste for Art Nouveau and Art Deco in the 1930s.

130 Local building firms were engaged in providing and maintaining Southport's housing stock. Surviving villas still contain woodwork, stained glass, and particularly plaster work of exquisite quality. The photograph is of the staff of a Forest Road decorator, which was typical of the many small building businesses in the town.

31 Providing services for the wealthy was the major source of income in Southport. The biggest single employer of labour was the local council. These road sweepers' carts were still to be seen in Southport after the Second World War.

32 The 'castles in the sands' were topped by forests of chimneys. Coal came into the town via the extensive Derby Road depot.

133a & b Although small industrial units proliferated behind the back streets of Southport, there was little in the way of large factories. An exception was Vulcan Motors, which moved from a small town-centre operation in Vulcan Street to a green-field site at Crossens.

THE·VULCAN·MOTOR
MANUFACTURING·CO·LTD.
NEW·WORKS·CROSSENS

Prescott & Dold, Architects
Wigan & Southport

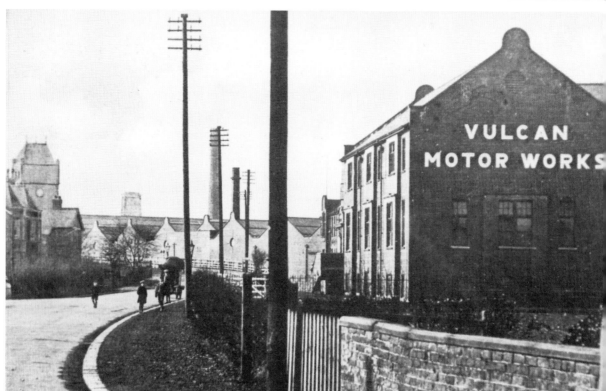

VULCAN
MOTOR WORKS

133c The scale of the enterprise is evident from the size of the building, and the celebration of vehicle number 1,000 on the line.

134a & b (*right and below*) The King's Gardens, opened by George V in 1913, replaced the fairground to the south of the lake. They extended to Pleasureland, which was fronted by colonnaded seating.

134c A 1915 photograph shows one of the stalls.

135a & b In 1914 a new Borough Engineer decided to use the town's rubbish as landfill to raise the level of the Lagoon area, which had been enclosed by the Marine Drive 20 years earlier. It was later converted into Prince's Park, which was opened by the Prince of Wales in 1921. This later featured a colonnade and was approached by an ornamental footbridge over the Marine Lake. On the seaward side a new open-air bathing pool was built in 1928. The whole sea-front area was a harmonious tribute to municipal planning and development.

136 In 1911, the Municipal Gardens were re-designed and two years later a circular copper-domed bandstand, which was to become synonymous with military band concerts, was erected.

137 Following advice from the sculptor, the statue of Queen Victoria was re-located at the top of Nevill Street.

138   The town's war memorial, which was consecrated in 1923, is of a scale unusual for a provincial town. It was regarded as the first part of a major new Town Planning Scheme for Lord Street. Built in Portland stone, it re-defined London Square with a tall central obelisk and two colonnades. The appeal fund rapidly reached the target of £30,000.

139   Further alterations to the Municipal Gardens included new light standards, and clusters of tall classical columns at the entrances.

140a The steam engine was used to demolish houses on Lord Street in order to create a site for the Palladium theatre/cinema.

140b The balustraded walls became a feature of the boulevard. The Mermaid was one of a number of fountains installed along Lord Street.

141 The *Prince of Wales Hotel* was built in 1876. Its location on Lord Street helped it to achieve a pre-eminent position amongst Southport's hotels. It was one of the first in the country to receive the approval of the Royal Automobile Club.

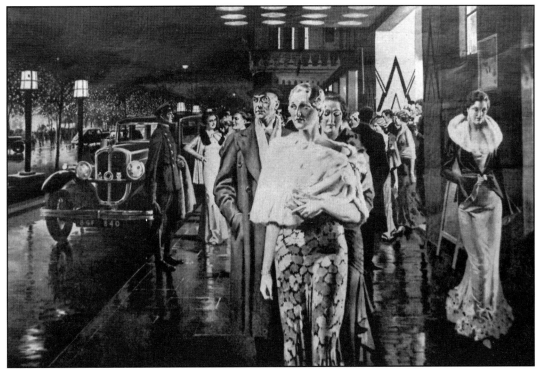

142 During the 1930s Fortunino Matania painted a series of publicity posters for Southport. 'Lord Street by Night', depicting patrons emerging from the Garrick Theatre, was used to publicise the town as a quality winter resort.

143 Motor sport quickly gained a following in the town. The Promenade provided a straight trials course of nearly one mile in length for the Southport Motor Club. Later meetings were held on the beach attracting crowds of up to 100,000.

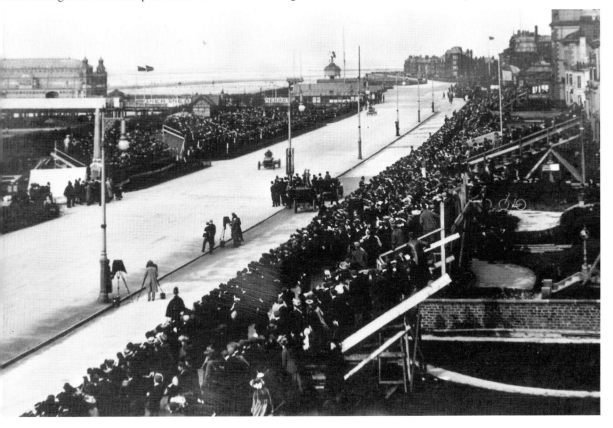

144 The Corporation was actively involved in promoting professional golf, a middle-class spectator sport. The Ryder Cup match with America was played at Southport and Ainsdale Golf Club in 1933 and again in 1937. The photograph shows play at the famous Gumbley hole.

145 Southport Flower Show is held annually in Victoria Park. It was inaugurated by the Corporation in 1924 and for many years the claim was made that it was the world's largest summer flower show.

146 The extensive extraction of beach sand for industry has introduced a new component to the landscape.

147 Fishermen still fish for Southport shrimps. The internal combustion engine has replaced horse-drawn carts, but the method of 'shanking' remains unchanged.

(*left*) Women making paper bags in Wm. Ashton's Tulketh Street workshop.

149 (*right*) Small workshops still abound, frequently amongst residential buildings. This garment manufacturer is typical of the scale of enterprise that can be found in and around the town.

150a Many of the 'castles in the sands', such as The Warren on a four-acre site in Westcliffe Road, have been demolished to make way for blocks of flats.

150b Others have been replaced by purpose-built nursing and residential homes, such as this example in Park Road.

150c Some, such as elegant Melton Grange in Cambridge Road, a building with listed elements, have been adapted for use as nursing homes.

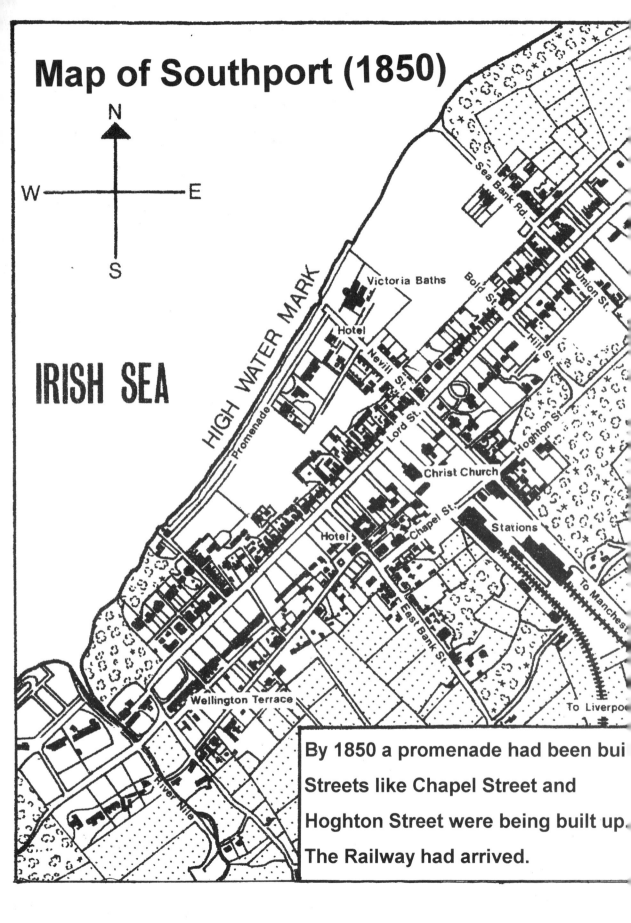

Map of Southport (1850)

N
W — E
S

IRISH SEA

HIGH WATER MARK

Promenade

Victoria Baths

Hotel

Nevill St.

Lord St.

Bold St.

Union St.

Hill St.

Sea Bank Rd.

Hoghton St.

Christ Church

Chapel St.

Hotel

Stations

East Bank St.

Wellington Terrace

River Nile

To Manchester

To Liverpool

By 1850 a promenade had been bui

Streets like Chapel Street and

Hoghton Street were being built up.

The Railway had arrived.